Amazing But True Dog tales

Bruce Nash and Allan Zullo

With Muriel MacFarlane

ANDREWS AND MCMEEL • *A Universal Press Syndicate Company* • KANSAS CITY

Designed by Rick Cusick
Illustrations by Paul Coker, Jr.

Nash, Bruce M.
    Amazing but true dog tales / Bruce Nash and Allan Zullo, with Muriel MacFarlane.
        p.   cm.
    ISBN 0-8362-8066-0 : $6.95
        1. Dogs—Anecdotes—Juvenile literature.   2. Dogs—Biography—Juvenile literature.
[1. Dogs.]   I. Zullo, Allan.   II. MacFarlane, Muriel.   III. Title.
SF426.5.N37 1994   94-25535
636.7—dc20   CIP

To Todd Schwartz, for proving that if you can dream it, you can do it.
— *Bruce Nash*

To Goldie, Bugaloo, Cleo, Winky, Dinky, TeeVee, Casey, Rocky, Spot, Tinkerbell, Chico, Toby, Tuffy, Heidi, Kelly, Janka, Star, Guido, Sammy, Mandy, Rosemary, and the unforgettable Sparky.
— *Allan Zullo*

Acknowledgments

There are several people who helped provide material for this book.

Special thanks go to Jessie Vicha, Fred Kirsch, John McGran, and the Delta Society for their cooperation.

We are especially grateful to all those owners who, in personal interviews, graciously shared with us intriguing accounts of their remarkable dogs.

Contents

Dogs have been our most loyal four-legged companions since the beginning of modern civilization...

Putting on the Dog

They are cheerful, brave, and faithful. They show us unconditional love, remarkable intelligence, and startling sensitivity. They are eager to play and even more eager to please. They ask for nothing more than a pat on the head and food in their bowl.

This book is a celebration of incredible canines whose antics and adventures will astound and amuse you. For example, Duke the thrill-seeking poodle rode on a roller coaster every day for six years. Mugsy the Jack Russell terrier was buried after getting hit by a car—and then shocked his grieving owners by showing up at the back door the next day. A golden retriever named Shanda is the top dog in Guffey, Colorado—because she's the mayor.

In our research, we found remarkable stories of canine heroes. For instance, Buddy the collie charged into a burning barn and shepherded one hundred frightened pregnant goats to safety. Sparky the yellow Labrador dragged his unconscious master, who had suffered a massive heart attack, an eighth of a mile back home to save his life. When her young master fell from a third-story building, Stella the German shepherd saved him by racing under him and cushioning his fall.

We also found some wacky accounts of dogs who wound up in big trouble. For example, Vegas the German shepherd shot her master in the back with a .22-caliber rifle—but she didn't mean to do it. Rocky the St. Bernard was arrested and thrown into the doggy slammer for five days on a shoplifting charge. And Wofford the golden retriever was cited for trying to check out a library book without a card.

Whether strays, purebreds, or mongrels, one thing is certain. These dogs are up to something amazing!

Heroic Dogs

...who rescued others

Dragged Out Drama

When his master suffered a massive heart attack and collapsed unconscious while on a walk, Sparky the yellow Labrador knew exactly what to do. He dragged his owner all the way home—an eighth of a mile away!

It happened on January 21, 1992, when fifty-one-year-old John "Bo" Culbertson, of Tullahoma, Tennessee, and his dog were heading home from their daily early-morning walk. Suddenly, Culbertson was stricken with chest pains and a tightness that quickly spread across his left shoulder.

"I began to black out," recalled the former coach and ginseng farmer. "Something was wrong and I didn't know what. As I started to fall down, I put my left hand under Sparky's choke collar, not wanting to lose him. I knew he was going to have to drag me. The last thing I remember was his tongue licking my face. Then all went black."

With Culbertson's hand locked in a death grip on his dog's collar, Sparky turned backward to minimize the tightening of his choker. Then he started dragging his owner up a lonely country road and straight to his home. It was no easy task. Culbertson tipped the scales at 227 pounds—outweighing the dog by more than one hundred pounds. Straining every step of the way, the muscular dog managed to pull Culbertson a distance of more than two football fields until they reached the front door.

Exhausted and panting, Sparky barked until Culbertson's wife Dotty opened the door. She was shocked by what she saw. "Bo's hand was under Sparky's collar," she recalled. "Bo's face was bluish. I could see he was still alive, but I feared he would die at any moment."

After prying his hand loose from the collar, Dotty put her stricken husband in the car and rushed him to the local hospital. He was then transferred to a Nashville hospital where he underwent triple bypass surgery. The heart attack starved his brain of oxygen and left him partially disabled.

"I asked the doctor what he thought would have happened if Bo had been out walking by himself," Dotty recalled. "He said Bo would have probably just sat down and died."

For his valiant effort, Sparky was named Ken-L Ration's 1992 Dog Hero of the Year.

"Sparky saved my life," said Culbertson. "He's worth millions to me. Anything Sparky wants, he's going to get."

Master-ful Rescues

In two recent cases, dogs saved a farmer and a rancher who were trapped underneath their vehicles far out in the boondocks.

In October 1993, seventy-five-year-old tobacco farmer Ken Emerson, of Vienna, Ontario, Canada, was operating his tractor in a field. Accompanying him was his grandson's dog, a German shepherd named Nellie. While the tractor was chugging along the side of a hill, it toppled over onto Emerson, knocking him out.

When the farmer regained consciousness, he was pinned beneath the tractor and badly injured. A worried Nellie remained with Emerson, licking his face. Realizing that if he didn't get help in a hurry he would die, the farmer tore off a piece of his shirt, gave it to the dog, and ordered her to go for help.

Gripping the fabric in her mouth, Nellie scampered to the front yard of Emerson's farmhouse. The dog dropped the fabric and stood over it, barking frantically. Moments later, Emerson's wife Pauline came outside and noticed the piece of her husband's shirt by the dog's paw.

Convinced her husband was in danger, she called for help and, following Nellie, found her husband barely alive. Emerson was rushed to the hospital where he recovered from leg and back injuries.

In a similar life-and-death situation, a bird dog named Jake helped rescue rancher Lou Dean Williams.

One summer day in 1993, Williams, forty-five, was out riding an all-terrain vehicle on her 750-acre horse ranch near Vernal, Utah, with her faithful brown-and-white dog. Miles from her house, the ATV broke down. As Williams tried to move it, she slipped and the 600-pound vehicle flipped over on her, pinning her legs. Jake, fortunately, managed to get out of the way.

Williams shouted for help, but she knew it was futile because no one was nearby. Jake, meanwhile, whined and barked because he could tell his mistress was in trouble.

"I shouted to Jake, 'Go home and get help!'" Williams recalled. She took off one of her gloves and tried to get him to take it home as a sign that she was in trouble. But for three hours, the loyal dog refused to leave her side.

No matter how hard she tried, Williams could not free herself. The pain in her legs intensified with each passing hour. Again and again, Williams implored her dog to run home for help.

Even though the worried dog didn't want to leave, he finally dashed off and ran back to the house where he found ranch hand Juan Morales. Jake growled and barked and pulled at the man's pants.

"At first I thought he wanted to bite me," Morales recalled. "But then I could see that he was a desperate-looking dog." When he finally realized that Jake wanted him to follow, Morales let the dog lead the way, and they soon came upon the injured rancher.

Said Williams, who suffered kidney damage and internal bleeding and nearly lost her legs, "You should have seen the hug I put on that dog."

On a bleak, cold day in 1987, Dorothy Rorex was taking a hike in the woods near Langley, Washington, with her Doberman pinscher Flicka. But the elderly woman twisted her ankle, fell, and cracked her hip.

Dorothy didn't panic. Instead, she tied her shoe to Flicka's collar and ordered the dog home. Flicka scampered to the house and barked frantically until Dorothy's husband realized that she was in trouble.

Following Flicka, Rorex found his injured wife covered with sticks and dirt, trying to stay warm until help arrived. Thanks to Flicka, Dorothy was rescued and later made a complete recovery.

Saved in the Lick of Time

Sable the hunting dog was born totally barkless, but that didn't stop her from warning her master that his house was on fire.

Late one night in the spring of 1991 in Somerset, England, a fire broke out in the kitchen of Stephen Helliar's wood-frame house. When the two-year-old mute mutt saw flames shooting up from the stove, she raced upstairs to Helliar's bedroom.

"Sable jumped up on my bed and started licking me," Helliar recalled. "I opened my eyes and saw the room was filling with smoke." Helliar bolted to the bedroom of his friend, Jane Lindsay, who lay unconscious and overcome by the thick smoke.

With Sable leading the way through the billowing, choking smoke, Helliar carried Lindsay outside where he revived her with mouth to mouth resuscitation.

"Sable should get credit for saving both the house and the lives of the two occupants inside," a Somerset fire official told reporters. "A few minutes more and the wooden structure would have been consumed by flames."

Said a grateful Lindsay, "It's still scary to think about. If it hadn't been for Sable, we would have died."

* * *

Maxine the Doberman was an abused nine-month-old abandoned in the woods when George Roeder found her and gave her a loving home.

Three years later, in 1988, she repaid the favor—by saving the lives of Roeder's two children in a destructive house fire. She had run back and forth through heavy smoke to awaken the two sleeping kids and lead them to safety.

The fire broke out at 3 A.M. in the second floor of the Roeders' house in Quakertown, Pennsylvania, while George, a truck driver, and his wife Deborah, a nurse, were at work. "Max woke me up," recalled fourteen-year-old George III. "She was jumping up on my bed, and she was whining and barking and pulling on me. When I woke up, I saw that my bed was on fire."

Maxine then dashed into the bedroom of twelve-year-old Jessica and yanked her out of bed. Through the choking smoke, the brave dog showed them the way to the stairs and out the front door. The blaze raged on and destroyed the second floor of the house.

"Without the dog, the children would have perished, there's no doubt about that," declared Quakertown fire chief Fred W. Guenst. "The dog absolutely saved their lives."

Added Dorothy Keith, of the Dog Club Federation, "This was something Maxine did to save her family. She was not trained in any way to do this. She did it because her instincts told her to save them."

Bucks County commissioners were so impressed by Maxine's bravery that they held a ceremony to honor her and proclaimed a "Maxine the Heroic Dog Day."

"The fire chief told me I owed Maxine a steak dinner," said Deborah Roeder. "I went to Ponderosa and bought her a big steak and that was her reward."

* * *

On a windy day in 1961, ten-year-old Penny Grantz, of Niles, Ohio, was burning some papers in the backyard when suddenly flying ashes ignited her skirt. The terrified girl began racing toward the house.

Meanwhile, the family dog, a collie named Duke, ran to Penny and seized the flaming skirt in his teeth. Then he tore and pawed the garment off of her and flung it to the ground. Despite suffering burns to his mouth, the dog barked loudly.

Penny's father, John, a night worker who was asleep at the time, heard the barking and dashed outside. By this time, the flames had spread to Penny's blouse. He ripped the burning clothing off his daughter and rushed her to the hospital where she remained for nine weeks.

"Had it not been for Duke's heroic actions, she probably would have died," said one of the attending physicians.

Thanks to his brave actions, Duke won the 1961 Ken-L Ration Dog Hero of the Year award.

* * *

Three years later, another collie won the same award for his courage in the face of fire. Buddy, a twenty-month-old purebred, saved nearly one hundred goats in a raging blaze that leveled most of his master's dairy farm in Budd Lake, New Jersey.

Early one morning in 1964, fire erupted in the farm's maternity barn. Buddy, smelling the smoke, began barking frantically outside until his owner Matthew S. Crinkley, Jr., looked out his bedroom window.

Dashing outside, Crinkley was astonished to see Buddy herding a flock of seventy expectant mother goats out of the burning barn. Despite severe burns on his paws and nasal damage from smoke inhalation, Buddy had maneuvered all the goats to safety by pushing them and nipping at their feet.

Thanks to the dog's warning, Crinkley was able to save a second barn which housed thirty more goats by wetting down the roof so sparks from the blaze wouldn't ignite the structure.

Said a spokesman for the Ken-L Ration award: "The one hundred goats, together with those since born of the expectant mothers, later constituted a flock of nearly three hundred goats that would surely have been lost had it not been for this intelligent and devoted collie."

Canine Cushion

When her eleven-year-old master plunged off the third story of a building under construction, a German shepherd mix named Stella saved the boy's life—by racing under him and cushioning his fall!

The dog's derring-do occurred in 1990 in Salerno, Italy. She was walking with her owner, Alfredo Iannone, and his friend when the boys decided to climb to the top of a construction site. Sensing danger, Stella refused to follow them up and kept barking warnings to the kids from below.

"Suddenly, I tripped and fell over the edge of the roof," Iannone told reporters later. "I was screaming my head off on the way down. I really thought I was going to die. Then my dog ran toward me like a bullet."

Stella dashed to the exact spot where Alfredo was about to hit—and, in an incredible display of selfless bravery, placed her body under the falling boy. "She threw herself between me and the ground," recalled Alfredo. "When I landed, it was like falling onto a mattress."

Although the sixty-five-pound boy plunged thirty-five feet, he suffered only minor bruises when he bounced off Stella. Amazingly, the heroic pooch was unharmed.

"Without that dog, Alfredo would be dead," declared Dr. Giorgio Sacchi, of the Salerno Public Hospital. "Stella is a hero!"

(Life) Guard Dogs

When Chris Georgiou fell into a fifteen-foot-deep pond wearing a heavy wool sweater, a thick coat, overalls, and boots, he thought for sure he was going to die. His clothes were dragging him down—and he didn't know how to swim.

But just as he was about to slip under the water for the last time, his two faithful dogs teamed up to save their drowning master from certain death.

Their remarkable rescue earned them special medals of heroism bestowed by the South Australian Canine Association.

In 1993, Georgiou, the sixty-six-year-old owner of a trout-fishing farm near Adelaide, Australia, was cutting tall grass along the bank of a large pond on his property. While Ziggy, his two-year-old Border collie, followed him wherever he went, his other dog, a two-year-old Rottweiler named Stella, was slumbering outside the house about sixty yards away.

Suddenly, Georgiou fell into the pond with a loud splash. "I was in fifteen feet of water," he recalled. "I'd never learned to swim a stroke and I could feel my heavy clothing weighing me down. It was as if I were wearing a lead suit and concrete boots."

11

Georgiou flailed his arms wildly, trying desperately to reach the bank. But he kept moving further out into the pond. Floundering to keep his head above water, Georgiou began to feel his strength seeping from him.

He shouted for help, but there was no one home or anyone near the pond. "I could hear Ziggy barking furiously," he recalled. "It was a shrill, frightened bark that I'd never heard before. I was coughing and sputtering. Finally, I couldn't fight anymore. I was about to go under for good. Then a miracle happened."

From out of nowhere, Stella—all ninety pounds of her—dove into the water and paddled straight to Georgiou. He grabbed her right hind leg and held on as she towed him slowly but steadily toward the bank. When they reached the shallow water, Georgiou let go, staggered up the side of the bank, and crumpled in a heap.

"The next thing I knew, the two dogs were licking my face and whining for me to get up," he recalled. "Then it hit me: Little Ziggy knew he wasn't strong enough to save me—he weighs only twenty-five pounds. So he had barked to Stella, who's strong as a horse, to come save my life.

"When I got home, I hugged the two of them and cried like a baby. I'd be a dead man if it wasn't for my dogs."

A Stroke of Genius

While his master lay paralyzed from a massive stroke, a Kelpie-Border collie named Trixie kept the elderly man alive by bringing him water until his rescue—nine days later.

In 1991, Jack Fyfe, seventy-five, of Sydney, Australia, suffered a stroke in his sleep that paralyzed the left side of his body. The retired florist lived alone with his six-year-old canine companion and wasn't expecting any visitors. He tried to get to the phone across the room, but he couldn't even roll out of bed.

"I'd never felt so helpless and afraid," Fyfe told reporters later.

As the temperature in his house climbed to ninety degrees, Fyfe feared that he would die from thirst. In his anguish, he cried out for water.

"Suddenly, Trixie bounded out of the room," he recalled. "I heard her drinking bowl scraping against the kitchen floor. Then she ran into the bedroom with an old bath towel hanging from her jaws. She had dipped the towel in her bowl, leaped onto my bed, and slopped the wet end of the towel against my face. With my good right hand, I pushed the end into my mouth and sucked the water out of it.

"Often I'd used the word 'water' in front of Trixie when I filled her water bowl. But for her to link this to fetching water for me seemed beyond belief!"

For the next four days, Fyfe said, Trixie periodically brought him a wet towel. But then her water bowl ran dry. "To my astonishment, she ran to the bathroom, dipped the towel in the toilet bowl, and then brought it back," he said. "I didn't care where the liquid came from. I thankfully sucked the water from the towel like a helpless baby."

Finally, Fyfe's nightmare ended on the ninth day when his daughter, concerned that she hadn't heard from him, entered the house and found the elderly man still lying on his bed.

Said Fyfe, who was able to walk again after extensive therapy, "I know that if my life is ever in danger again, Trixie will be there for me."

Dynamic Duo

Two lovable house dogs helped save the life of their severely injured mistress as she lay bleeding to death.

On the morning of December 2, 1991, Andi Troast, fifty, went outside in an old housecoat to feed the herd of deer and flock of wild geese that regularly visited her rural home near Paupack, Pennsylvania. Andi slipped on some ice and, in a freak accident, snapped her right foot nearly in two. "I screamed so loudly, the poor animals scattered in all directions," she recalled.

Back in the house about one hundred yards away were her two dogs, a sheepdog mix named Rufus and a Chow Chow named Teddy Bear. No one else was home.

"I was alone in the woods and no one was due back soon, so I realized that my survival depended on me and my dogs," said Andi. "The blood steadily was flowing out and I knew I had to get into the house to phone for help."

With pain shooting up from her bleeding, nearly-severed foot, Andi inched on her back over the frozen ground until she reached the front steps of her house. "I was getting weaker by the second and I was losing consciousness," she recalled. "The door was closed and the handle was out of my reach.

"Rufus was barking and tearing at the glass on the storm door. I yelled, 'Come on, Rufus, open the door! Uppy-up, uppy-up, push the knob.' He started hitting the latch with his nose and paws and suddenly the door flew open."

Both dogs came outside. On Andi's command, Teddy Bear, who weighs fifty pounds, sat still and used her body to prop open the door. Meanwhile, Rufus scooted next to Andi. "I grabbed for his collar and managed to get my arms fully around his hairy neck and I told him, 'Pull Mommy inside the house, Rufus.'"

Even though Andi weighed about three hundred pounds, the determined, loyal one-hundred-pound dog managed to drag her over a fifteen-inch doorstep and into the dining room where she phoned for help. Then Rufus and Teddy Bear cuddled with their mistress, keeping her warm until paramedics arrived. "Rufus kept licking me in the face to keep me awake," she said. "The dogs gave me such comfort. Their undying affection and loving care kept me alive."

Doctors were able to save Andi's life and foot although it took more than a year before she could walk again. Throughout her recuperation, her dogs would walk beside her to assist her in case she lost her balance. "Rufus still helps me up from the chair or couch, and helps carry the laundry for me," said Andi.

"If it wasn't for my dogs, I wouldn't be here today."

Free Willy

A nine-year-old weimaraner named Willy saved his mistress from deadly poison gas.

In 1992, Betty Souder, of Los Alamos, New Mexico, had gone to sleep unaware that her furnace was leaking deadly carbon dioxide, a colorless, odorless gas. But Willy sensed the danger.

"I was asleep when he started to whine and paw at me," recalled Betty. "He refused to stop. So I said, 'Willy, stop it! Lie down and go to sleep.' I wanted to roll over and get back to sleep. But Willy kept whining and pawing me, so I dragged myself out of bed, thinking he needed to go outside."

When Betty stood up, she felt dizzy and sick. But she still had no idea that the deadly gas was invading her house. She opened the door and let Willy out, but he immediately wanted to go back inside. He was acting strangely and kept weaving while he walked.

Feeling sicker by the minute, Betty tried to call for help. She was so weak and disoriented that twice she dropped the phone before she could dial. Then, with Willy by her side, she staggered out of the house.

"As soon as we got out into the cold fresh air, my head cleared up," Betty said. "Willy too was back to his old self. He knew enough to wake me from a sleep that could have been my last."

Catch of a Lifetime

A black Labrador dived into a tidal pool and snagged a drowning toddler and pulled him to safety.

One day in 1991 at a seaside park in Wales, two-year-old Arron Wines had wandered away from his picnicking parents. Suddenly, he tumbled into a tidal pool and was floating face down in the water.

No one saw him at first. But a black Labrador named Tess did. She was walking with her owner, Heather Hodder, when she broke into a run and started barking wildly.

"Tess dived straight into the water and I suddenly realized she had a hold of a little boy's body," Heather told reporters later. "She dragged him out by his trousers. The child's lips were blue and he wasn't breathing."

Arron's parents, Dean and Cherie Wines, and his uncle, Clive Oram, heard Heather scream and raced to the beach. They gave the little boy mouth-to-mouth resuscitation until he was breathing on his own again.

After his son recovered from the ordeal, Dean Wines said, "There's no doubt my son would be dead it wasn't for that heroic dog. She was wonderful and I can't thank her enough."

* * *

In 1987, Stephanie Winfield, three, of Riverton, Wyoming, wandered away from her backyard when her mother's back was turned. Stephanie walked to a nearby irrigation canal, fell in, and began desperately thrashing to keep from drowning.

Seconds later, the family dog, a Rottweiler named Katz, barked frantically and then plunged into the canal. The dog grabbed Stephanie by the blouse and pulled her to the edge of the canal.

Once she had dragged the little girl safely back onto the bank, Katz kept barking. Stephanie's frantic mother followed the sound of the barking to the canal where she found her daughter sitting in wet, ripped clothes with Katz by her side.

Katy's Big Splash

When Mary Meredith fell unconscious into a full bathtub, her face slipped under the water. She was minutes away from drowning when her dog, a retriever named Katy, splashed into the tub, nuzzled under Mary's chin, and propped the woman's head above the water until she regained consciousness.

In 1991, Mary, forty-eight, of Ipswich, Suffolk, England, was climbing out of the tub when she lost her balance, fell, and hit her head. She blacked out and slumped back into the water face first. Her nose and mouth went under the water as blood dripped from her head injury.

Meanwhile, Katy was downstairs when she heard a thud. She bounded up to the bathroom, nosed open the door, peered into the tub, and saw her mistress floating.

Katy hated baths so much that until that moment she had refused to go near the bathroom whenever her mistress took a bath. But sensing that Mary was in trouble, the whimpering dog jumped into the tub and slid alongside Mary. Then the dog pushed her head into the water and eased her body underneath Mary's chin until Mary's mouth and nose were above the water.

Gradually Mary regained consciousness, gagging and coughing up water. When she opened her eyes, she realized that Katy was under her chin, keeping her head above the water.

"I held on to Katy and told her, 'I don't know what I'd have done without you,'" recalled Mary. "I owe my life to her. She's a very special dog."

Pooch Patrol

Among the most heroic dogs are those who sense danger on roads, streets, and curbs and save their unsuspecting owners from potentially fatal accidents. For instance:

Six-year-old Alaina Fawcett, her two sisters, and her mother were waiting for the school bus in St. Mary, Ontario, Canada, one day in 1992. Nago, the family's 145-pound Akita, was facing the opposite direction when he saw a truck skid on a patch of ice and head straight toward the unsuspecting Alaina.

Without hesitation, the brave dog jumped in front of the truck and pushed Alaina into a ditch, then leaped out of the way a split second before the vehicle skidded past them.

For his heroism, Nago was inducted into the Ralston Purina Canada Animal Hall of Fame. "Nago is a hero," said the girl's mother. "Alaina would have been hit if it hadn't been for him."

* * *

Sherrie McKeehan, who is partially deaf and lives alone, owns a springer spaniel named Shep who was trained by Paws With A Cause to assist her.

But what Shep did to save his mistress's life was not something for which he was trained.

The two were driving along a Michigan highway in 1991 when Sherrie began feeling extremely sleepy. "The next thing I knew, Shep was in my lap, nudging me," she recalled. Her car had veered into the grass median and was heading toward oncoming traffic when the dog woke up his mistress and she braked just in time.

"I can't explain how Shep knew we were in danger," said Sherrie, "but thank God he did."

* * *

In 1968, Ringo, a St. Bernard mix, followed his little two-and-a-half-year-old master, Randy Saleh of Euless, Texas, who had wandered away from home.

When Randy's mother realized he was missing, police immediately began searching for the boy. About two hours later and three-quarters of a mile from the Saleh house, traffic came to a standstill on busy and dangerous Pipeline Road. More than forty cars in both directions were stopped by what many people thought was a mad dog.

It was Ringo, resolutely stationed in the center of the road, blocking cars and even leaping against their fenders to keep them from moving. Just a few feet away was little Randy, innocently playing in the roadway as he had been doing for nearly fifteen minutes.

Motorists looked on in wonder as the dog, after stopping a car, would rush back to the child and nudge him to the side of the roadway. But the little boy, apparently thinking it was some sort of game, would immediately scurry back to the center of the highway and sit there, laughing.

The frantic Ringo kept up his efforts to prevent his master from being hit by a car. Finally, motorist Harley Jones cautiously approached the dog and calmed him down enough to permit Jones to pick up the boy and carry him off to the side of the road.

Ringo's efforts earned him an award as the Ken-L Ration Dog Hero of the Year.

* * *

An earlier winner, a collie named Tang, saved children from being run over or injured by vehicles in the 1950s—in five separate incidents.

Owned by Air Force Captain Maurice Dyer and his family, Tang first displayed his strong protective instinct for children at an air base in Alaska. As speeding military trucks rumbled past the homes of air force personnel, Tang would keep children away from the road by barking and blocking their path. Twice he had to push kids safely away from the paths of fast-moving vehicles.

When Captain Dyer was transferred to Denison, Texas, the collie continued to act as a street patrol guard for the neighborhood children. Again, he saved the lives of two more kids who had wandered into the path of oncoming traffic by shoving them out of the way.

One day, Tang planted himself squarely in front of a parked milk delivery truck. When the milkman put the truck in gear, the dog refused to budge. Tang just kept barking. The puzzled milkman got out of the truck and looked around. He finally discovered the reason for the dog's strange behavior.

A two-year-old girl had climbed into the back of the dairy truck and was standing by the open rear door. Had the truck moved forward, she almost certainly would have fallen out onto the street. Once the girl was safely in the arms of her mother, Tang quit barking and let the dairy truck continue on its round.

On the Right Track

Tara the German shepherd saved the life of an injured stranger who was lying unconscious across a railroad track minutes before a freight train sped by.

In 1991 near Duncan, British Columbia, Canada, a twenty-three-year-old motorcyclist was racing up the middle of the tracks when he lost control. He fell and landed between the rails, cracking his helmet in two places and suffering severe head injuries. The biker was sprawled helplessly in the path of a train due to come barreling down on him in forty-five minutes.

Fortunately, Tara, owned by farmer Helmut Langer, was ambling near the tracks when she spotted the injured motorcyclist. She immediately galloped home to get help.

"Tara came leaping up the stairs and right into our bedroom," recalled Langer. "I was really angry with her because she knows it's a no-no to come up the stairs." He ordered her to leave but she followed him around the house, whining, turning in circles, and barking.

"Finally, I gave up and said, 'Okay, Tara, I'll follow you, but this better be good,'" said Langer. "I never saw the dog act like that before, so I figured it must be something important. In fact, as we walked, she kept turning around and making little circles to make sure I'd follow her."

When the man and his dog reached the edge of the farm, Langer spotted the injured motorcyclist. "I knew the afternoon train was coming through in less than an hour and would make mincemeat of the guy if we didn't get him out of there. The train never would have been able to stop. There's a curve before the farm and the fellow lying there never would have been seen by the engineer."

When paramedics arrived, they treated the biker on the scene and transported him to the hospital where he eventually recovered. "Doctors said he would have died if Tara hadn't found him so quickly after the accident," said Langer. "Cops and the ambulance people petted her and told her how wonderful she was—and I think she understood our appreciation. I turned to Tara and told her, 'Tara, you're fantastic! You saved a man's life. You're a wonderful dog.'"

The Noah of Dog Heroes

A courageous American pit bull terrier named Weela helped save thirty people, twenty-nine dogs, and thirteen horses from perishing during killer floods in southern California in 1993.

Heavy rains had turned the normally placid Tijuana River into a raging, muddy torrent near the Mexican border. Weela's owners, Lori and Daniel Watkins of Imperial Beach, California, decided to check on the dozen dogs—including seven puppies—that lived on the ranch of a hospitalized friend in the flooded valley.

"When we got there, the water had risen so high that the dogs were crowding on top of a couple of bales of hay about a half-mile away from us," Lori recalled. "The water was waist deep in spots and we faced quicksand, dangerous drop-offs, and mud bogs. We weren't sure how to reach the dogs at first. But Weela knew. She's just a house dog but she seemed to have this ability to sense where it was safe for us to walk, so we just followed her.

"We finally reached the dogs, and they were scared to death and a couple of them were in shock. It took my husband and I and my cousin Carol Kasper two trips and about six hours to bring them all out safely with Weela leading the way."

A week later, the sixty-five-pound, seven-year-old red pit bull once again came to the rescue when the valley was hit with another flood that left thirteen hungry, frightened horses stranded on a manure pile about a half-mile from dry land.

"We knew the horses needed to be saved, but again we couldn't find a safe path to bring them food," said Lori. "But after the way Weela performed when we rescued the dogs, we had full faith in her to show us the safest route.

"The ground was unstable and the water was dangerous, but Weela just knew where to go. She went way upstream and found a way for us to get to the horses and bring them food. Weela helped carry the hay in her own backpack.

"Every day that we went out there, Weela had to find a new path for us because the river kept changing. Finally, when the water went down four days later, we were able to get the horses out. But I had to order Weela to stay far behind the horses so she wouldn't spook them. She looked at me as though her feelings were hurt."

A short while later, Lori discovered that seventeen dogs—including a female Dalmatian mix and her thirteen puppies—were trapped and starving on an island made by the second flood. Like before, the water, mud, and quicksand made it dangerous to reach the animals. But, once again, Weela found a safe path for the rescuers to follow.

"We couldn't get too close to the dogs because they were so frightened," said Lori. "About every other day, we would bring them food and leave it. Weela carried her own backpack of thirty to fifty pounds of dog food for them. Sometimes we put the food on an inner tube and let her pull it across the mud and water to the island. Because the river changed, she had to keep finding new routes for us to get there."

After a grueling month of slogging through the treacherous mud and water with Weela in the lead, the rescuers managed to save all the dogs, some of which needed immediate medical attention. "We brought most of them home with us," said Lori, "and found them good homes. While the dogs were here, Weela became very possessive of the puppies, licking them and curling up with them."

Incredibly, after helping rescue dogs and horses, Weela saved more than two dozen people from a potential tragedy.

Lori and her family were on the same side of the river when they came upon a group of thirty Mexican men, women, and children who were getting ready to cross the floodwaters.

"It looked like an extremely dangerous spot," recalled Lori. "None of us could speak Spanish and none of them could speak English. Suddenly, Weela took off running until she was between them and the water. Then she barked and kept running back and forth parallel to the bank and refused to let them cross there. She then led them, and us, to a shallower spot upstream where we all safely crossed to the other side. If she hadn't been there, I'm convinced that many of them would have been swept away and drowned.

"We're very proud of Weela. She was constantly willing to put herself in dangerous situations to make sure that we had a safe path. She's a great dog."

For her extraordinary actions, Weela was named the 1993 winner of the annual Ken-L Ration Dog Hero of the Year award.

Attack Dogs

Dogs have risked their lives to save their masters from deadly animal attacks. For instance:

Grizzly Bear the St. Bernard was aptly named. He saved the life of his mistress when she was attacked by a menacing grizzly bear.

One day in 1970, Mrs. David Gratias, who owned and operated a lodge with her husband in Denali, Alaska, heard a strange noise outside. Leaving the door open to her cabin where her two-year-old daughter was sleeping, Mrs. Gratias went to investigate with Grizzly Bear by her side.

She discovered a bear cub in the backyard. Knowing that the mother must be near, Mrs. Gratias went back to the front yard and came face to face with the female grizzly. The eight-foot-tall beast raised up to attack. As Mrs. Gratias tried to flee, she slipped and fell. In a flash, the bear raked the woman's cheek with one claw while slashing her shoulder with the other.

The bear leaned over to take a possible fatal bite when it suddenly staggered back. The courageous 180-pound Grizzly Bear had charged into the animal. Roaring with rage, the bear tried to attack Mrs. Gratias again. But the St. Bernard wouldn't let it. Making sure he stayed between his mistress and the bear, the dog clawed and bit the grizzly.

Bleeding badly from her wounds, Mrs. Gratias passed out while the battle between bear and dog waged on. When the injured woman finally regained consciousness, Grizzly Bear was licking her face. The bear and cub had disappeared and, although the cabin door was still open, her daughter was still sleeping soundly inside.

Although the dog was spotted with blood, no wounds were found and authorities assumed the blood came from the bear. Mrs. Gratias eventually recovered from her injuries and remained forever grateful that Grizzly Bear had saved her from a grizzly bear.

* * *

A German shepherd named Fawn risked her life to save a three-year-old boy from a deadly rattlesnake bite.

In 1975, Russ "Tiger" Schoenberger was visiting the home of his grandparents, Mr. and Mrs. William Schlesinger of St. Petersburg, Florida, who owned four dogs, including Fawn. While Tiger was playing in the backyard where three of the dogs were napping, Fawn was inside a screened porch with the Schlesingers.

Suddenly, Fawn sensed danger. She pushed open the screen door, bounded into the backyard, leaped on Tiger, and knocked him down. The shocked little boy quickly got up and Fawn pushed him down again. Only then did he realize why. Just a few feet away, a deadly four-foot-long diamondback rattlesnake was coiled and ready to strike.

The brave dog pounced on the snake and kept it away from the boy. While Fawn battled the reptile, Tiger's grandfather grabbed a gun and shot the rattler, but not before it had sunk its fangs into the dog. Although Fawn hovered near death for several weeks, she made a complete recovery.

* * *

Early one morning in 1985, farmer Al Choate, of Port Townsend, Washington, and his thirteen-year-old Border collie–Australian shepherd mix named Tango went to check on two newborn calves.

While Choate was examining one of the calves, its protective mother charged Choate from behind. She smashed into his back with her head and then butted him in the chest, breaking several of his ribs and puncturing a lung.

Seeing his master attacked, Tango leaped into action. He bit into the cow's jaw and held on until his injured master could crawl away. Once the dog knew that Choate was safe, he let go of the cow.

Choate recovered from his injuries and Tango was not harmed.

* * *

One day in 1957, two-and-a-half-year-old Dawn Hecox was playing in the yard on the family farm in Timewell, Illinois. The little girl decided to get a better look at some baby pigs that were in a fenced-in enclosure.

But when Dawn crawled through the fence, the mother sow became infuriated. The pig charged the girl and knocked her to the ground and began biting and mauling her.

Hearing Dawn's screams, the family dog, a collie named Blaze, ran to her rescue. With a single bound, he cleared the fence and tore into the sow. The enraged pig then began battling the dog. Blaze continued to fight until he was sure that the badly injured girl had escaped.

Then he leaped back over the fence and stayed with his little mistress until her parents swept her up and took her to the hospital. Dawn, who was in critical condition for two days, was hospitalized for three weeks. When she finally came home, the first thing she did was give Blaze a big hug of thanks.

Snow Job

Villa, a one-year-old black Newfoundland, was a big, lovable family pet who one memorable day astounded people with her courage and intelligence in saving the life of a girl during a severe blizzard.

It happened in 1983 when next-door neighbor Andrea Anderson, eleven, of Villas, New Jersey, was playing in the snow near her house. Suddenly, the wind gusted up to sixty miles an hour and drove her backward. Andrea fell down an embankment and into a large snowdrift. She tried to free herself, but she was trapped up to her chest in the heavy snow. Andrea yelled for help, but the shrieking wind drowned out her desperate cries.

Moments earlier, Villa, owned by Dick and Lynda Veit, had been let outside to romp in the snow in their enclosed backyard. When the dog heard Andrea shouting for help, she sprang into action. Villa climbed a five-foot-high fence and made her way through the drifting snow until she reached the frightened, trapped girl.

After trying to comfort Andrea with a few licks on the face, Villa circled her several times, tamping down the snow next to her. Next, the one hundred-pound dog stood in front of Andrea so she could grab her. With the girl's arms around Villa's neck, the dog backed up and yanked Andrea free from the snowdrift.

By now, the wind-driven snow had reduced visibility to near zero. But Villa, with Andrea holding onto the dog's neck, slowly led the girl safely home.

A Leap of Faith

A collie mix named Woodie helped rescue a friend of her mistress's—by leaping off an eighty-foot cliff.

On a summer afternoon in 1980, Woodie was walking with her owner, Rae Anne Knitter, and the woman's fiancé, Ray Thomas, along a nature trail in the Cleveland

Metroparks Rocky River Reservation. Ray, an amateur photographer, wanted to capture the spectacular view from atop a steep shale cliff. While Rae Anne and Woodie waited several yards away on a path, Ray positioned himself for the shot at the edge of the cliff.

Suddenly, Woodie began twisting and tugging on her leash, trying to yank free from Rae Anne. Believing that something was wrong based on the actions of the usually well-behaved dog, Rae Anne let go of Woodie. The dog raced up the path and disappeared.

When Rae Anne reached the edge of the cliff, neither Ray nor Woodie were in sight. Then Rae Anne leaned over the side and gasped in horror. There was Ray, lying face down and unconscious in a stream eighty feet below. And right by his side was Woodie!

Rae Anne quickly realized that her fiancé had lost his footing and plunged over the side. Incredibly, Woodie had bravely jumped herself just to be by his side. The leap fractured both of the dog's hips. But despite the pain, she struggled to get next to Ray. Then she put her head under his chin and lifted his head out of the water.

Within minutes, rescuers arrived and carted off the injured man and dog. Ray spent two months in the hospital, undergoing treatment for multiple fractures in his back and arm. Woodie, who suffered internal injuries in addition to the broken hips, fully recovered.

For her amazing bravery, Woodie was named Ken-L Ration Dog Hero of the Year. "Woodie is more affectionate than ever," Rae Anne said at the awards ceremony. "It's as if she realizes how lucky she is to be alive."

Naughty Dogs
...who landed in trouble

Gunning for Trouble

A dog shot her master right in the back with a rifle—but she didn't mean to do it.

The bizarre shooting happened in 1991 in St. Laurent, Manitoba, Canada, shortly after Joe Petrowski, thirty-two, had cleaned and adjusted the sight of a long-barreled .22-caliber rifle. Working in his backyard, Petrowski had removed the wooden stock and the metal guard underneath the trigger and fastened the weapon to a portable workbench. The back end of the rifle, including the exposed trigger, extended out from beyond the workbench.

As Petrowski began shooting at a target thirty yards away to test the sight, his year-old German shepherd, Vegas, was by his side.

"After my final shot, I reloaded the rifle and went to check the target," Petrowski recalled.

Meanwhile, Vegas walked under the back end of the rifle that jutted out from the portable workbench. The top of her back brushed against the exposed trigger. The gun went off at the exact moment that her master, who was facing the target, was directly in the line of fire.

"I heard the click," Petrowski recalled. "I knew it was coming, but there was no time to duck. I felt the bullet smash into my body. It fractured four ribs and tore up my liver and my stomach. I blacked out for about thirty minutes. When I finally opened my eyes, I realized that Vegas was pawing at my face and chewing on my neck."

Because no one else was home at the time, the bleeding Petrowski knew he had to get help for himself if he was going to survive. He managed to get back to the house and phone for help. "Every breath was a struggle," he said, "but I told them what happened because I didn't want the police to think there was some gunman waiting in the yard."

Despite the pain and critical injuries, Petrowski still kept his sense of humor. "The gal on the phone didn't believe me when I told her the shooting involved a dog," he recalled. "So I told her, 'Don't worry, the dog doesn't know how to reload.'"

Petrowski was hovering near death when the volunteer paramedics arrived and rushed him to the hospital, where he was in critical condition. After several operations and a lengthy recuperation, Petrowski made a full recovery.

"For two or three months after the shooting, Vegas couldn't stand to see him lie down alone," said Petrowski's wife Cindy. "Vegas would nip at him so he couldn't go to sleep. I think she was afraid that he wouldn't ever get up again. At night, she stayed by his side when we went to bed. In fact, she sleeps at the end of the bed now."

Petrowski doesn't blame Vegas for shooting him. "I made a serious mistake putting myself in front of a loaded gun," he said. "It was a bad judgment call. Some people asked me if I wanted to kill Vegas. And my answer was 'Why?' She didn't do anything wrong."

Constable Luc Monette, of the Royal Canadian Mounted Police, who investigated the freak accident, said he found dog fur by the trigger. "It was a pretty strange shooting—one in a million."

At Least He Didn't Get the Book Thrown at Him

A golden retriever named Wofford loves to sink his teeth into a good book—literally.

Unfortunately, his penchant for literary works landed him in court.

Wofford, owned by David Viccellio, of Norfolk, Virginia, has a thing about books. "Our family likes to read, so there are books everywhere," explained Viccellio. "Whenever a guest comes over, Wofford will pick up a book with his teeth and hand it to him. He just loves books, especially paperbacks." Other times, the book hound will curl up in a corner with a good book.

One day in 1993, the dog slipped through a broken slat in the backyard fence and saunstered over to the Larchmont branch library next door. The back door had been left open to catch a breeze, so Wofford trotted inside. Seeing all those books, Wofford couldn't resist taking one.

He snatched a children's book off a little table and, being a friendly pooch, headed over to where the people were—at the checkout counter.

"There he was, standing by the desk," recalled Albert Ward of the library staff. "Waiting very patiently. Behaving like you should in a library."

After doing a double-take, one of the librarians called the phone number on Wofford's collar, hoping to talk to the owner. But no one was home. "I got a message on my answer machine that said, 'This is the library. Your dog is trying to check out a book and he doesn't have a card,'" recalled Viccellio. "In fact, the librarian left several messages and finally they called the animal control people."

Viccellio arrived moments before Wofford was going to be hauled off to the pound. The owner was handed the dog—and a summons to appear in court for having a dog at large and not having a dog license.

"I showed Wofford the summonses, and they got his attention," said Viccellio. "He was burying bones out in the yard. I guess he felt we weren't going to feed him if things went badly in court."

When Viccellio appeared before Judge William Oast, the judge read the details of the case and asked him, "Was the dog trying to take a book out of the library?"

"No, your honor," said Viccellio. "He wasn't taking it. He was in the checkout line when they found him."

"Well, that's good to hear," said Oast.

The understanding judge didn't throw the book at the dog. Instead, he dropped the charges against Wofford, but ordered Viccellio to pay court costs of $28.

Reading about the zany case in the newspapers, students at an elementary school in Virginia Beach, Virginia, gave Wofford a gift—his very own school library card.

Make No Bones About It, He's a Shoplifter

Rocky the St. Bernard was arrested and thrown in the slammer for five days on a charge of shoplifting.

On January 7, 1991, the 175-pound dog was pacing back and forth in front of the entrance to the RXD Pharmacy in Gloucester Township, New Jersey. With sad puppy dog eyes, Rocky kept staring inside at the customers and employees.

Dianna Hodson, who worked in the store, couldn't bear to watch the dog shivering in the frigid weather. "He was out in the cold so long that I just had to let him inside," she told reporters.

Once inside, Rocky warmed up and casually walked up and down the aisles until he stopped at the pet food section. Then he saw something that had him drooling—a ninety-nine-cent, two-pound bag of Pet Pleasers rawhide bones. The pilfering pooch picked up a bag and then ambled out an automatic door while customers stood and watched in amazement.

"He stopped in the pet food section at the bag of Pet Pleasers like he was reading it," declared store supervisor Tony Pepe. "Then he picked it up in his big jaws and he was gone."

Pepe immediately called the police, who cornered Rocky a few yards from the store. But the dog thought the police just wanted to play and he kept dodging them. Not until the dog catcher showed up did Rocky finally surrender.

"The suspect was definitely resisting arrest," said Sgt. Kenneth Saunders, who helped collar the crook. "He didn't actually confess, but he still had the stolen goods with him. We can't read a dog his rights, so we handed him over to the Animal Orphanage."

The St. Bernard was held at the shelter for five days until his owner claimed him. Kind-hearted officials dropped the charges once they learned that Rocky had wandered away from home two weeks earlier and had become lost. They were convinced that he had swiped the bones solely because he was hungry and not because he was a canine criminal.

Dial 911-DOG

A playful puppy got collared by the cops after he summoned them—by accidentally dialing an emergency number on the telephone.

The five-month-old mutt, named Ben, was home alone in Higham, England, in 1993 when, for fun, he knocked the phone to the floor and began chewing on it. As he gnawed away, Ben randomly tapped out the emergency number with his paws.

The operator who answered heard heavy breathing and a dog barking on the other end of the line. Thinking a victim was hurt and unable to speak and that the dog was yelping at an attacker, the operator notified police.

When the call was traced to the house, a policewoman went to investigate. She peered into the window and saw the phone on the floor with blood on it, so she called for additional backup.

Within minutes, eight more cops arrived. But because the house was locked, police used a sledgehammer to smash in the front door. They rushed inside—only to discover Ben sitting in the corner, wagging his tail. Police then realized the blood on the phone came from the teething dog's gums.

The cops gave Ben a pat on the head and then announced the case was closed.

Diamond in the Ruff

For a few hours, Duque the mutt was worth $15,000. That's how much the diamond ring was valued when he swallowed it in one gulp.

In 1991, Carolyn Solomon took her cherished ring to Creative Jewelers in Laguna Beach, California, to have it cleaned. Greeting her at the door was Duque, a friendly sixty-pound black mixed breed owned by jeweler Art Peltz.

Duque loved it whenever Peltz had to clean jewelry because the dog would always jump up and nip at the steam which sprayed out of the ring-cleaning machine. "Duque's antics are so legendary that people come to the store just to watch him snap at the steam machine," said Peltz.

On this particular day, Duque got carried away. When Peltz held Carolyn's ring and waved it through the steam, Duque jumped up to take a bite of the spray—and gulped down the ring.

"I was cleaning Carolyn's ring," recalled Peltz, "when I told her, 'One day he's going to eat a ring. . . . Oh, oh, I think he just did.' I couldn't believe my eyes when the ring disappeared."

Added Carolyn, "We always thought it was so cute the way the dog reacted to the steam. But when he swallowed my diamond, I didn't think it was so funny."

Once she recovered from the shock that her valuable piece of jewelry was now in the dog's stomach, Carolyn took Duque to an animal hospital and asked the vet for help. "I wasn't going to let that dog out of my sight," she recalled. After taking an X-ray that showed the ring was in Duque's stomach, Dr. James Levin gave him a drink that made the dog throw up—and out flew the ring.

Peltz cleaned the ring again—but this time he made sure that Duque stayed in the front of the shop.

The Bark Was Worse than the Bite

Davey, a pit bull terrier, attacked and chewed thirteen trees on city property, causing $1,200 in damages.

But it wasn't his fault. He was only following orders.

In 1988, police discovered that several young trees in downtown Lancaster, Pennsylvania, had been severely damaged. An investigation eventually led authorities to Davey. While he was held harmless, his owner's nineteen-year-old nephew was arrested. At the trial, the teen's attorney said the youth was showing off the dog for friends. "It was much like having a dog fetch a stick," said the lawyer, "except that the stick was stationary."

Although Davey got off scot free, the teen was sentenced to two years probation and forty hours of pruning and planting city trees for issuing the dog's search-and-destroy orders.

A New Leash on Life

No condemned dog generated more news or cost so much in legal fees than did Taro.

Authorities wanted to put Taro to death for mauling a dog and biting a girl. However, his owners fought back in a valiant effort to spring him from death row. It took more than two-and-a-half years, a $100,000 legal battle, a nationwide television poll, and a reprieve from the governor to spare the life of the two-year-old, 115-pound, brown-and-white Akita.

Taro's troubles began in May 1990, when he fought with a neighbor's twenty-five-pound Welsh terrier. The little dog was so badly hurt that it had to be put to sleep. Officials charged Taro's owners, Lonnie and Sandy Lehrer of Haworth, New Jersey, with having a vicious dog.

Then seven months later, before that case was resolved, Taro wound up in more trouble. Authorities claimed he bit the lip of the Lehrers' ten-year-old niece Brie who was visiting their home.

Sandy denied the charge, telling reporters, "Brie kept pulling Taro's curly tail, saying she wanted to straighten it out, and he kept running from her. Later that night, Brie came running out of the bedroom crying with a cut on her lip. We took Brie to the hospital and the doctor maintained she'd been bitten.

"But we think Brie was teasing the dog and when he tried to push her away, one of his nails caught her lip and cut it. Taro loves children."

But in January 1991, authorities said the incident was further proof that Taro was indeed vicious. As a result, the dog was taken away from the Lehrers and put on death row—a kennel at the Bergen County Jail. Under New Jersey law, when a dog is declared vicious, it must be put to sleep.

But the Lehrers refused to accept the verdict. They fought Taro's case in the New Jersey court system, costing them more than $25,000 in attorney's fees. Meanwhile, the city of Haworth spent $60,000 in the legal battle and Taro's jailers shelled out $17,000 on the dog's upkeep.

When the case looked bleak, Sandy Lehrer turned to the media for help. Wearing a "Free Taro" T-shirt, Sandy generated scores of newspaper articles in New York, New

Jersey, and across the nation. The TV tabloid show "Current Affair" aired several sympathetic stories about Taro's fate. Producers even conducted a nationwide phone-in poll of viewers on whether they believed Taro should live or die. The results were overwhelming—viewers, by a nine-to-one margin, wanted the dog's life spared.

Finally, in January, 1994—two and a half years after Taro first landed in trouble—he got the big break that his owners had fought so hard for. In one of her first acts as governor of New Jersey, newly elected Christine Whitman pardoned Taro. But the governor attached two conditions: The dog had to leave the state for good and be handed to new owners who were willing to assume all future liabilities.

On March 1, 1994, Taro was freed from jail and given a new leash on life. Said Sheriff Jack Terhune, "We were kind of sad to see him go. He was a model prisoner."

Caring Dogs
...who helped those in need

Paws to Give Thanks

Although guide dogs have been serving the blind for generations, only recently are people with other disabilities relying on four-pawed assistants—with amazing results.

"A lot of people don't even know about these kinds of animals," said Linda Hines, executive director of the Delta Society, a national group that promotes awareness of the way animals help humans. "We can show you proof positive that animals change people's lives."

Among the Delta Society's 1993 canine winners for their remarkable skills and ability to help people were Joe the assist dog, Ivy the guide dog, and Chelsea the signal dog.

Joe the Assist Dog

Susan Duncan wouldn't know what to do without her faithful dog Joe. He's more than just a pal. He helps his handicapped mistress get out of bed in the morning, brings her the phone when it rings—and even assists with the grocery shopping and banking!

Susan, a married Bellevue, Washington, health education teacher with two children, was stricken with multiple sclerosis in 1978. The nerve disorder worsened until she needed a cane and sometimes a wheelchair. She has since struggled with poor balance, muscle weakness, and reduced stamina.

In 1990, she trained the family dog, Casper, to help fetch her cane, carry packages, and do other simple chores. But then he died unexpectedly. "I was not willing to go back to the way it had been," she said. So in 1991, Susan visited the local Humane Society shelter and found Joe, a 107-pound, part–German shepherd, part–Great Dane stray who was only days away from being put to sleep. "To greet me, he put his paws up on my shoulder. I fell in his water bowl, and he sat on top of me."

It was the start of a beautiful friendship.

Susan personally trained the loving dog, who has given her freedom as she copes with her ever-worsening MS.

In the morning, when Susan is at her weakest, Joe removes the bedcovers. The dog gently grabs Susan's pajama legs in his mouth one at a time and pulls her feet off the edge of the bed. Susan then swings to a sitting position. Joe opens the dresser drawers and takes out whatever items of clothing that Susan points to and gives them to her.

Whenever the phone rings, Joe grabs the receiver, which has a long cord, and brings it to her.

Often times, Susan falls down, but Joe is always there to help her. He squats down so she can put her arm around his shoulder. Then Joe stands up, which pulls Susan part-way up, making it easier for her to stand.

Joe assists with the banking. After Susan punches in the numbers on the automatic teller machine, Joe opens the money door and grabs the greenbacks in his mouth. "I won't let him punch the numbers," she said. "If I told him my code, he'd clean me out."

Remarkably, Joe also helps Susan with the grocery shopping. She points to items she wants and he grabs them with his mouth. Susan then puts the items in a backpack that Joe wears that can hold up to thirty pounds of food.

"Joe keeps me more functional and increases my accessibility," said Susan. "And he decreases my reliance on other people. He's taken a lot of heat off my family.

"Everybody thinks I gave Joe a second chance by rescuing him from an animal shelter," Susan told reporters. "But Joe gave me a second chance at life, too."

Ivy the Guide Dog

When blind rehabilitation counselor Toni Eames discovered that her cherished guide dog Flicka had only a few months left to live, she was heartbroken.

She knew she needed a new guide dog, but didn't want to wait until Flicka died. So Toni brought in a new dog, a year-old golden retriever named Ivy, to help her and the dying Flicka.

Ivy quickly fell in love with Toni and befriended and gradually assumed the older dog's duties as Flicka's health declined. When Flicka died in 1983, Ivy expertly took over her role.

"One of the first things Ivy learned was how to manage on the Long Island Railroad," said Toni, who lived in New York before moving to Fresno, California. "Even now, if we're getting on an Amtrak train, she goes in front of all the other people and I say, 'You have to excuse her. She's from New York.'"

Twice Ivy has saved Toni from danger. Once, when Toni and Ivy were waiting in a crowded subway station, a despicable fellow passenger told her that the train was in the station and was boarding, when in fact it hadn't even arrived yet. Toni would have walked right off the platform to almost certain death had Ivy not refused Toni's forward command.

Another time, Toni and Ivy were crossing a busy New York street when Toni lost her footing on an icy patch and fell. Ivy immediately stood between his mistress and an oncoming car which managed to swerve out of the way.

"You learn never to question your dog," she said. "If you do, that's when you get into trouble."

Ivy went above and beyond the call of duty when Toni's husband, who is also blind, was without his guide dog because the animal was recuperating from surgery.

"My husband's dog had cancer and had his leg amputated, so in the course of recovery Ivy had a dual role," said Toni. "She guided him in a different style. And Ivy was the other dog's motivation to get going again.

"Ivy and I have had a full and happy life. And I appreciate and treasure each day we have together."

Chelsea the Signal Dog

Chelsea, a Belgian sheepdog, does double duty as a signal dog for a hearing-impaired married couple.

Since 1987, she has served as the ears for Paul Ogden, professor of deaf education at California State University–Fresno, who's been deaf since birth, and his wife Anne, who is hard of hearing.

"He's been a vital part of our family," Ogden said through sign language. "Chelsea hears for us."

Chelsea was trained by Canine Companions for Independence to alert her master to such sounds as a doorbell, an alarm clock, an oven buzzer, and a smoke alarm. She responds to fifty-six commands, given either verbally or with hand gestures. But unlike working dogs who wait for a master's commands, signal dogs must make judgment calls. They must sort out incoming sounds from background noise and determine what is important. "Chelsea must make decisions such as alert the master or let it pass," said Paul.

"She's wonderful in the morning, waking me very gently with her cold nose pressed against my face. If I don't get up, she paws me a few times, and if I continue to ignore the alarm clock, she jumps on the bed."

She also helps the Ogdens communicate with each other. "Since Anne and I cannot yell through walls to one another, we use Chelsea as a messenger service, sending notes to one another," said Paul.

"Chelsea is really a tribute to the freedom we enjoy."

Wheelchair Dogs

When paraplegic Cyndi Irish goes for an outing, she hitches up her two dogs to her wheelchair.

Cyndi, who lives near Fairbanks, Alaska, has been paralyzed from the waist down since breaking her back in a motorcycle accident in 1982. But she hasn't let her disability stop her from enjoying the raw beauty of the countryside.

She simply attaches chains from her wheelchair to harnesses for her black German shepherd Max and her mixed-breed husky Girl Dawg—and off they go.

"It's exhilarating," Cyndi said. "It's my version of taking a brisk walk. "This is rugged country. You learn self-reliance early in the game or you don't survive."

Canine Counselors

Slick the German shepherd–golden retriever mix doesn't have a college degree, but she's still a full-time staff member of a facility that comforts families in crisis.

"She relies on instinct and a big heart to help others," said her owner, Kay Darst, manager of Hospital Hospitality House in Kalamazoo, Michigan. The old mansion provides a home away from home for families of seriously ill or dying patients.

"People who are under intense emotional stress often find it hard to talk about their troubles to strangers," said Kay. "But many times, those same people can talk with Slick. She listens without passing judgment. She's there to offer them support.

"She knows long before I do if someone is crying in their room. One time, a woman whose child was dying quietly went up to her room. Slick knew she was upset and went upstairs and put her head on the woman's lap. Later, the woman told me she had been crying her heart out and it helped to have Slick there with her.

"Slick is particularly good with men because generally they don't openly talk about their feelings. One time, a young man had to decide whether or not to remove life support from his forty-two-year-old mother. He couldn't bring himself to talk about it with anybody. So he took

Slick up to his room and then took her for a long walk and talked it out with her. When they returned, he decided to let his mother die naturally without life support.

"Another time, an older man was faced with the same decision about his seriously ill wife. He and I sat at the kitchen table over coffee. But rather than talk to me directly, he poured out his feelings to Slick. He patted her and talked to her and Slick sat there with her head on his knees and listened. The man felt so much better afterward. That happens a lot around here with Slick."

Sometimes Slick offers the temporary residents of the house a chance to release some of the emotional stress that builds up after a long day at the hospital. "People will wrestle with her or play Frisbee with her or even take her for a run just to relieve the stress," said Kay.

Kay believes Slick knows how to touch the hearts of troubled families because the dog was once down and out, too. "In the winter of 1987, my son found her abandoned in a garbage bin in the back of a supermarket when she was only five weeks old," she said. "She turned into such a sweetheart. When I took the job as manager of Hospitality House in 1989, she came with me because we're a team.

"People get real attached to her and they often bring her treats, like chicken breasts and Big Macs. Sometimes we'll get a donation and a note attached asking that some of the money go to buy Slick a bone."

* * *

When school counselor Bob Hollinbeck needed an assistant, he didn't have far to look. He "hired" his loving Labrador retriever Coco.

Despite his obvious lack of academic credentials, Coco became an instant success with the kids at Eisenhower Grade School in Hopkins, Minnesota.

The black Lab wears a name tag that reads "Assistant School Counselor" and her picture hangs in the hallway with photos of other members of the school staff.

Hollinbeck said that Coco fills an emotional void for many of the school's 650 students. "It's tough being a kid," the counselor told *People* magazine. "Sometimes they just need Coco to be there for them—not to talk, not to lecture, just to be there. And this dog accepts you, whether you have the Nikes or not, whether you're male or female, rich or poor. It's unconditional love, and a lot of kids don't get that anywhere else."

Coco is so popular that students sign up days in advance for the privilege of walking her. The canine counselor works without pay, except for a daily treat.

"She helps the kids, just like a teacher or some other adult would," said a sixth grader. "She's a pretty cool dog."

Coco often seems to sense when a child needs a sympathetic look, a wagging tail, or a wet lick. "One child was upset, ashamed about something he'd done in class," Hollinbeck recalled. "He wouldn't talk to his teacher, but he said he'd talk to Coco. I left the room. He talked with the dog, then he was able to talk to the teacher.

"Coco sure is one special dog."

Oriented to Lead the Way

A Seeing-Eye dog named Orient went on the hike of a lifetime—he guided his blind master along the entire 2,144-mile length of the Appalachian Trail.

In March, 1990, Bill Irwin, fifty-one, strapped on a ninety-pound backpack and set out from Dahlonega, Georgia, with his trusted German shepherd leading the way. "Orient was no doubt wondering why in the world we were so far away from his bed and food bowl," said Irwin.

Despite sores on his back early in the arduous trip from carrying a heavy pack of his own, Orient plodded along without whimpering. He helped his master along mountain paths, across rain-swollen streams, and around boulders and fallen trees. When Irwin set up camp at night, Orient curled up close to him and barked whenever he heard wild animals rustling nearby. Together they slogged through rain, mud, and wind. They endured freezing temperatures, sweltering heat, and biting insects.

Finally, after eight grueling, exhausting months, Orient led his master safely to the end of the trail. Said Irwin, "He was my compass, my friend, my companion."

Never-Say-Die-Dogs

...who cheated death

A Grave Situation

In at least two recent cases, pooches have come back from the grave—literally.

On an October afternoon in 1990, a four-year-old Jack Russell terrier named Mugsy was hit by a car in front of the house of his owner, Viola Tiszl, of Severna Park, Maryland. Although Viola was not home at the time, her boyfriend, Glenn Maloney, was there taking care of her children, Megan, five, and Kevin, three.

As soon as he heard the screeching of the tires, Maloney looked out the window and saw that Mugsy had been struck. He told the kids to stay in the house and then he dashed outside to see if the dog was still alive. "I picked Mugsy up, but he died in my arms," he told reporters later.

Maloney carried the body to the backyard and dug a

hole three feet deep and buried Mugsy. "I know a dead dog when I see one," he recalled. "This one was real dead. He was not breathing. He had no heartbeat."

That evening, after she came home from work, Tiszl and Maloney took the children out back to view the grave. Megan said a prayer and the family decided to put a wooden cross on the burial site the next morning.

But then at 5:30 A.M.—about fourteen hours after Mugsy had been buried— Tiszl and Maloney were awakened by a scratching noise at the back door. "I went to the door and I couldn't believe it," recalled Maloney. "There was Mugsy with his little tail wagging ninety miles an hour!"

Mugsy was covered with dirt and his eyes were bloodshot, but otherwise he seemed in excellent shape.

Tiszl attributed the dog's astounding recovery to his breeding. "Jack Russells are bred to burrow after foxes," she said. "I guess when he woke up in that hole, he just thought it was another old hole. He dug his way out, not knowing it was supposed to be his grave."

* * *

Four years later Brownie, a small, tan mutt, also made a dramatic return from the "dead."

Owned by Mary Bratcher of Artesia, New Mexico, the dog had fallen asleep behind a pickup truck. Not knowing Brownie was there, Mary backed up the truck and ran over him.

Breaking down in tears, Mary lifted her limp pet and looked for any sign of life, but she found none. "His chest went up and down twice and then he stopped breathing," recalled Mary. "I thought he was dead."

Not wanting her children to see their lifeless dog, Mary had her brother carry Brownie to a nearby field and bury the beloved pet in a three-foot-deep grave. "I told the kids that Brownie had gone to heaven," said Mary.

Late the next afternoon, Mary returned from a trip to the store and screamed in shock. Lying by the front porch steps was none other than Brownie himself! He was shivering from the cold, caked in dirt, and not breathing very well. Mary rushed him to the veterinarian, who treated the dog for a rib injury, a broken leg, and a concussion. The most serious problem was that Brownie lost his right eye. But otherwise, he made a full recovery.

When the dog returned home, he was given some special treats and a new nickname—Lazarus.

Cheating Death by a Whisker

Looie the Maltese poodle missed his own cremation by only a whisker.

One snowy night in 1990, the frisky, black, eight-year-old pooch managed to squeeze out of the backyard gate of the home of his owner, Martin Heimlich, of Salt Lake City. As Heimlich chased after him, the dog darted into a busy street and within seconds was struck by a minivan, then by a car, and finally by another auto.

The horror-stricken Heimlich dashed out into the heavy traffic and picked up his lifeless, bloody dog. The owner checked his dog but could not detect any breathing or a heartbeat.

"The whole family was in shock," recalled Heimlich. "We were grieving, certain that we'd lost Looie."

He planned to bury his pooch, but record-low temperatures had frozen the ground. So he put Looie in a box outside on the porch and called the animal control office to pick up the dog and cremate him. The dog was left in the box for two days.

"On the morning his body was to be picked up, I couldn't resist taking one last peek," said Heimlich. "So I opened the box and he looked up at me. I said to myself, 'Dead dogs don't look up at you.' Then he wobbled his head. And I said, 'Dead dogs don't move.' I reached down and found his heart was pounding and he was warm."

Thrilled beyond belief, Heimlich took Looie to the Central Valley Veterinary Hospital where the dog was operated on for a fractured hind leg, ruptured ear drum, and eye injuries. Although he lost his left eye, Looie recovered from his near-tragedy.

"Looie just refused to die," said Heimlich. "Obviously, it wasn't his time to go."

The Dog with Nine Lives

Roadie the coonhound obviously doesn't know that only cats are supposed to have nine lives, not dogs.

The miracle mutt was hit by a train, lay helplessly between the tracks for three days as dozens of trains roared over him, suffered the loss of two legs, and twice faced attempts to shoot him. Yet, incredibly, he survived.

"He has a heart as big as all outdoors," said Dr. Mike Griffitt, the veterinarian who saved the dog. "He deserved a second chance."

Actually, Roadie avoided death time and time again.

Roadie's ordeal began in November 1992, when he was hunting with his owner in the woods near Nicholasville, Kentucky. While chasing a raccoon onto nearby railroad tracks, Roadie was struck by a freight train. His owner, who had lost sight of the dog when the canine took off after the raccoon, searched for Roadie without success.

Despite being hit by a train, Roadie clung to life. For three agony-filled days, the bleeding dog lay between the rails, unable to move because his left front leg and right rear leg had been horribly mangled. More than fifty trains passed over him, but he survived because he was laid out flat between the rails. If the pitiful pooch had raised his head, a train would have cut him to pieces.

A railroad worker spotted the critically injured dog and tried to end his suffering. The man pulled out his pistol and squeezed the trigger, but the gun jammed.

"When the man got home that night, he tested his pistol and it fired the first time he pulled the trigger," said Dr. Griffitt. "I guess Roadie wasn't meant to die."

The railroad worker summoned the police who, in turn, called Dr. Griffitt. "When I got out there, the dog was lying between the tracks with his head on the ground," recalled the vet. "He was the most pitiful sight I've ever seen and it brought tears to my eyes. Two of his legs were shredded. It was raining and cold. He was gray from the grease, dirt, and soot of the trains passing over him. I've treated animals for fifteen years. But I've never seen anything as sorrowful as that dog."

While most frightened, injured animals snarl, Roadie wagged his tail when Dr. Griffitt approached him. "I thought, 'This dog must have a tremendous will to live,'" said the vet. "He was so happy to see me. There was no way I could put him to sleep after all he'd been through."

Dr. Griffitt gingerly picked up the dog, drove him to the clinic, and called the owner listed on the dog's collar. When the owner arrived, he took one look at Roadie and said he would take the dog home and shoot him to put him out of his misery.

"I put the dog in the guy's truck," recalled Dr. Griffitt. "As I walked away, I turned and looked back at him one more time. The dog looked at me and wagged his tail. That did it. I couldn't let him go."

Dr. Griffitt talked the owner into letting him keep the dog. The first thing the vet did was give the coonhound the name Railroad, or Roadie for short. The next day, Dr. Griffitt amputated the dog's two mangled legs and nursed him back to health. Amazingly, within a week, the pooch was back on his feet—all two of them.

"Roadie can do anything he wants to—run, play, jump up into your lap," said the vet. "He can even jump into my truck and run as fast as any four-legged dog."

When a local newspaper ran a feature about Roadie's incredible ordeal, animal lovers sent cards and letters, and even money. People stopped by the clinic just to see him. "Roadie loves everybody," said Dr. Griffitt. "He's happy all the time—and he's so pleased to be alive."

* * *

Roadie should meet Trainwreck. Incredibly, on almost the same day as Roadie's near-fatal injury, a year-old German shepherd was hit by a train and left for dead for a week in the snow—but he too made a miraculous recovery.

An engineer on the commuter train that runs between South Bend and Michigan City, Indiana, reported that his train had struck and killed a dog. The presumedly dead animal lay in a snowbank for a week.

But when another engineer, Ted Nekvasil, rode past the dog, he was shocked to see the animal was still alive. "He had somehow pushed himself up on his front legs, but his back half wasn't moving," Nekvasil recalled. On his return trip, Nekvasil actually stopped his passenger train to check on the dog. He found a weak, emaciated German shepherd that could barely move. The engineer notified the dispatcher to get help for the dog and offered to pay the costs of the rescue.

Two railroad workers, Bill Reshkin and Steve Pollack, volunteered to help the dog. When they reached him, the injured dog slowly wagged his tail and let them carry him in a blanket. They brought him to an animal clinic in Michigan City where they were met by Nekvasil and veterinarian Dr. Christine Ellis.

After examining the dog, taking X-rays, and checking blood work, Dr. Ellis found no broken bones or internal injuries. "I still didn't think he had much of a chance of survival," she recalled. "I thought about putting him to sleep. He had been comatose and lying in the cold for a week and was suffering from hypothermia. His muscles had atrophied. But then he lifted his head, looked up at me with those big trusting eyes, and wagged his tail. That's when I thought, 'We can't let him die without giving him a chance.'

"He began eating and we worked with him every day with his therapy to stretch out his muscles. He was so accepting. He never complained even though the therapy had to hurt."

Dr. Ellis believes that when struck by the commuter train, the dog had received a glancing blow to the head that left him unconscious. Ironically, lying in the snow and cold probably saved his life, she said. The cold slowed down his metabolism, allowing him to survive for the week. Had it been warm, he probably would have died from dehydration.

Dr. Ellis gave him the name Trainwreck because every day she would enter the clinic and ask, "How's my train wreck dog?"

It took Trainwreck weeks, but he eventually was able to walk again. After efforts to find his owner proved futile, he was given a new home on a farm near Michigan City.

"He's such a sweet, loving dog," said Dr. Ellis. "He touched all our hearts. We're delighted that he's doing so well now."

A Modern-Day Toto

Like Toto in the classic movie *The Wizard of Oz*, Sadie the Yorkshire terrier was sucked into the sky by a vicious tornado and dumped down alive—two miles away.

On September 13, 1993, Sadie was playing in the yard alone while her owners—James and Sandra Davis of Saginaw, Texas—were at work. Suddenly, a twister roared through the neighborhood and slammed into the Davises' house.

Minutes later, the Davises rushed home and discovered that their house had sustained heavy damage, later estimated at $60,000. But their first concern was for Sadie, a Christmas present given five years earlier to their daughter Lindsay when she was three.

"When we first came home and saw all the pieces of fence and roof and decking all over the place, we started pulling pieces up looking for Sadie," recalled James.

Then the Davises searched around the neighborhood, but still couldn't find her.

"One of our neighbors came up to me and asked what was I looking for," recalled Sandra. "I told her Sadie and she asked, 'Was it brown and white?' I said, 'Yes.' And she said that she had seen the tornado pick up a brown and white furry ball. When it was twenty feet in the air, she realized it was a little dog. My heart just sank."

When they learned Sadie had been carried off by the twister, the Davises feared the worst—that she had been killed. But they also hoped that she had survived the tornado. So the Davises combed the countryside, but they failed to find any sign of her.

However, the next day, their despair turned to joy. They received a call from a man who had found their four-pound terrier safe and sound shortly after the storm, wandering by the side of a road—two miles from her home. Luckily, the dog had been wearing a name tag with the Davises' phone number on it.

Except for a few ant bites, Sadie appeared to be none the worse for wear.

"We were so thrilled when we got her back," said James. "She's like a member of our family. Surviving that tornado was nothing short of a miracle."

The Dogs that Refused to Die

Each city has suffered its share of horror stories—senseless, cold-blooded abuse of animals. But occasionally out of these sickening, outrageous cases come amazing accounts of canine survival that deeply move pet lovers.

Tramp and Timex were dogs that beat death and, in doing so, unleashed an outpouring of love.

On May 3, 1991, Tramp was left on a forty-foot chain in the yard so the neighborhood kids could play with the five-year-old, fifty-pound mongrel while his owners, Cameron and Sally Wright of Indianapolis, were at work.

Sometime during the day, a fiendish neighbor took the chain that was connected to Tramp's collar and attached it to the back bumper of a pickup truck. Then the sicko got into his truck and dragged the helpless, yelping mutt for nearly a mile before the dog slipped its collar.

Sadly, Tramp lost nearly all of his skin and suffered serious street burns over half his body. One of his eyes was nearly gouged out and the pads of his paws were scraped raw. But the plucky pooch managed to make it back home fifteen minutes after Sally had returned from work.

"He was just a pitiful sight," recalled Sally. "He looked like a piece of raw meat."

Sally rushed her injured pet to veterinarian Dr. Sandra Norman, who recalled, "It was the worst case of road burns I've seen. Sometimes you sense an animal will give up and just die. Tramp was not that kind of dog."

Sally quickly learned from a friend that a neighbor had dragged Tramp behind his truck. "You could see blood marks on the road," Sally recalled. "We measured it later and found it was eight-tenths of a mile." The neighbor was arrested and later convicted on charges of cruelty to animals and malicious damage. He was sentenced to sixty days in jail, two years' probation, eighty hours of community service, and fined $500. The neighbor has since moved away.

Meanwhile, the gutsy pooch underwent thirteen operations, needed five hundred stitches to close his wounds, and remained in intensive care for three weeks. "It was touch and go those first few weeks," said Sally. "He was at the vet's for six weeks and it took him nearly a year to fully recover."

As word of Tramp's plight spread, thousands of animal lovers in Indianapolis rallied behind the dog and donated $13,000 to pay for his hospital care. "People were just great," said Sally. "They brought him roast beef and flowers and toys." Tramp rewarded their love by pulling through.

"Best of all, Tramp is still friendly with everyone," said Sally. "He acts as though nothing had ever happened."

★ ★ ★

Less than two years later, in February 1993, Timex, a mixed-breed terrier, won the hearts of Texans after he was beaten so mercilessly that he couldn't even crawl and was left to die in a pool of blood.

The savagely battered dog was found barely alive in a construction firm's parking lot in Mansfield, Texas. "He was hit at least a dozen times over the head with a board or bat," recalled James Bias, executive director of the Humane Society of North Texas. "Then he was thrown over a six-foot-high barbed wire fence around the lot. You could see where he hit the ground, dragged himself a few feet, and collapsed."

Timex was so bloody that when animal rescue workers picked him up, they couldn't tell that he was white with tan markings.

"What got us was how he'd taken this beating and wasn't showing any signs of viciousness," said Bias. "He didn't make any fuss when we handled him. He just peered up at us with his little puffed-up face. We were so moved and we all vowed we had to save him."

Timex was rushed to the Benbrook Animal Hospital near Fort Worth, where he underwent several operations to repair his wounds. "He had head trauma, a badly damaged eye, and fractured teeth," recalled veterinarian Dr. Cynthia Jones. "He was in such bad shape. But I knew he'd make it because even though he was so hurt, he still wagged his tail. We treated him for about a month. He lost an eye, but otherwise Timex made a miraculous recovery. I've never seen a dog beaten so badly that survived."

While he was recuperating, Texas newspapers carried daily stories about Timex. Texans, touched by his battling spirit, sent him hundreds of gifts and get-well cards— and donated more than $6,000 for his medical care. "One person even cooked a turkey and deboned it and dropped it off here for Timex to eat," said Dr. Jones. So many people called to check on his condition that the animal hospital had to set up a special phone line to give updated recorded messages on his progress.

"He touched the hearts of so many people," said Dr. Jones. "This dog represented the idea that every animal deserves a chance."

More than two hundred families offered to adopt the stray dog. Once he made a full recovery, animal care officials found Timex a loving family. "He's been doing just great," said Dr. Jones. "He's spoiled rotten."

So how did he get his name? Explained James Bias, "We named him Timex because he'd taken a licking, but he kept on ticking, just like those old Timex watch commercials used to say."

The Waterlogged Seadog

Santos, a Belgian canal-barge dog, slipped off a yacht at sea and wasn't discovered missing until the next morning. His grief-stricken owners presumed he had drowned.

Boy, were they in for a surprise!

The small, frisky, black pooch was the pet of Peter and Dorothy Muilenburg and their son Diego—a family who loved sailing to different ports of call along the Caribbean and South American coasts aboard their ketch, *Breath*.

Santos was a schipperke whose ancestors were bred to serve aboard barges in Belgium. The dogs would swim ashore in the canals and nip at the heels of slow tow horses. The dogs also would bark if anyone fell overboard.

When the Muilenburgs first got him, they worried that maybe he didn't belong on a boat. Before he was three months old, Santos had almost drowned twice. Once, while running down the deck, he shot right off the boat. His owners heard scratching on the hull and discovered the dog treading water.

Then a month later, while the boat was anchored offshore, Santos accidentally plunged into the water again, and the ebb tide carried him out to sea. A startled skin diver found him paddling in the ocean.

But once he outgrew puppydom, Santos managed to stay topside and avoid further unplanned dunkings—until that fateful night in 1991 when he slipped and fell overboard five miles off the Venezuelan coast.

The Muilenburgs didn't miss him until the next morning after they had anchored at Puerto Azul. They went ashore to report their heartbreaking loss to the port captain who was busy supervising a sport-fishing tournament. He offered no encouragement, but promised to keep an eye out. The couple then went to a nearby bar and reminisced about their beloved pet and how much they would miss him.

Wrote Muilenburg in *Sail* magazine, "'Oh, well,' I consoled Dorothy. 'With that dog's temperament, we were lucky to have him as long as we did.' Dorothy's eyes brimmed. 'He was such a dear little dog. To think of him out there all alone!' A tear started down her cheek.

"Then we heard a shout from the port captain. 'You won't believe it,' he said. 'I just called the fishing boats on the radio to tally their standings for the scoreboard. And the last boat said they caught nothing—except a little black dog!'"

Someone on board the boat had spotted Santos bobbing in the ocean and scooped up the dog with a hand net.

"Back on *Breath*, Santos received a joyous welcome and got his own helping of the family dinner," said Muilenburg. "But his eyes were glazed as if they'd seen the whole of his life pass before them, and right after supper, he crashed."

Muilenburg wondered whether Santos's brush with death would make a more sensible animal of him. The next day, the skipper got his answer. Seeing kids playing on the beach with a German shepherd, Santos leaped into the sea and paddled toward the action.

Hard to Swallow

Some dogs will eat anything—including cue balls, golf balls, and even knives!

A devilish dog had her cake and the cake knife, too. In 1994, a nine-month-old, thirty-three-pound Border collie puppy named Apple wanted to satisfy her sweet tooth. When she saw a devil's food cake sitting atop the kitchen table, she couldn't resist. She wolfed down a large piece of the cake—along with a foot-long carving knife that had been left inside it.

Owner Eric Fuchs, of New York, was away, but his roommate Claudio Fernandez discovered what the bad Apple had done and rushed her to the Animal Medical Center. In a delicate two-hour operation, veterinarian Dr. Elaine Caplan removed the knife, repaired some internal damage caused by the blade, and stitched up a thirteen-inch incision.

"Apple is a very lucky dog," said Dr. Caplan. "She swallowed the knife handle-first. If she'd swallowed it blade-first, she wouldn't have survived."

* * *

Nike the German shepherd had a ball almost every time he went with his owner to the golf course. And that posed a problem because the dog was gulping down whole golf balls—a whopping twenty-four, to be exact.

In 1988, owner Robert Hoffman, of Latham, New York, began bringing Nike with him when he went to the practice tee. Eventually, Hoffman noticed that the seven-year-old Nike was not feeling well and took him to the animal clinic. There, the veterinarian discovered the problem. He wound up removing two dozen "ballstones" from Nike's belly and she made a complete recovery.

Hoffman continued to take Nike with him to the driving range, but he curbed the dog's appetite by spraying repellent on his golf balls.

* * *

Eric the Great Dane proved he was a real pool shark—by gobbling up a cue ball during a pool tournament.

Eric had a penchant for stealing cue balls in the pool room of the Woodcutter's Pub, owned by his master Fred Lundberg, of Dorset, England. But the dog always spit the balls out whenever Lundberg ordered him to do so.

However, during a 1993 tournament, Eric snatched a cue ball off the table and swallowed it. After giving the players a spare ball to finish their match, Lundberg took the dog to the animal hospital.

"I wasn't sure whether to put Eric on an operating table or a pool table," joked veterinarian Dr. Guy Wolverson, who successfully removed the cue ball from the dog's stomach.

As for Eric, he ended up in the doghouse. Lundberg banned him from the pool room.

High Dives

Paco the dog took one misstep—and plunged eleven stories from a condominium balcony. Yet, amazingly, the next day, the pooch was greeting visitors as though nothing had happened.

"It was quite a feat," declared owner Frank Woods, of New Smyrna Beach, Florida. "We began calling him 'Wonder Dog.'"

One day in 1993, the fluffy, white, ten-year-old bichon frise, who was virtually blind from cataracts, was lounging with Woods on the balcony of his oceanside condo. But while sniffing the sea air, Paco stepped through a balcony railing to what Woods feared was certain death. "I saw the tail go over," recalled Woods. "I thought it was all over then."

The fifteen-pound dog slammed onto his side when he hit the ground. But, fortunately, the soil had been softened by a recent heavy rain. To the surprise of condo residents who witnessed Paco's plunge, the dog was still alive.

They quickly sought the help of Volusia County lifeguards Mark Brown and Curt Szabo, who were nearby. "I'm a canine lover myself, so I thought we'd do what we could to help him," Brown told reporters. The lifeguards fashioned a stretcher from a leg splint meant for humans.

Then Woods rushed Paco to Dr. Andy Mozlin at the Smyrna Veterinary Hospital. Despite the 110-foot fall, Paco suffered nothing more than a broken leg and a bruised bladder. He was treated and released eight hours after the accident. "He landed on his side, so that spread the impact out," explained Dr. Mozlin. "It's incredible, but he left here with his tail wagging."

Added Brown, "Especially since he's blind, Paco must have gotten a heck of a rush dropping eleven floors."

* * *

Guinness the bird dog took a dive from twice as high—off a cliff on the British coast.

In 1991, Guinness was walking with his human family, the Dightons, of Edenbridge, England, near the edge of a huge seaside cliff. "Suddenly, Guinness went racing past me, chasing a bird," ten-year-old Barry, Jr., recalled. "I couldn't stop him."

The spaniel went sailing off the cliff, which rose 225 feet from a rocky beach below.

When he discovered what had happened, Barry, Sr., fearfully looked over the edge, expecting to see Guinness's broken body on the rocks below. But, luckily, the pooch had landed smack into the English Channel and was still very much alive. He had begun paddling toward shore when two startled fisherman, who saw his fall, plucked him from the water and returned him to his much-relieved owners.

What saved Guinness from certain death was the tide."He was lucky it was high tide," said Barry, Sr. "He could never have survived those rocks."

Nevertheless, the 225-foot plunge into the cold water still left Guinness with injuries. The dog was taken to the animal clinic where he was treated for internal bleeding and a damaged lung. However, he made a full recovery.

Meanwhile, the Dightons vow never to walk near a cliff again with Guinness.

Lost and Hound

For three and a half years, Lucas, a hound from South Carolina, was lost in the brutal Canadian wilderness and given up for dead, presumed fatally mauled by a bear.

But then one day, long after his owner had lost hope of ever seeing the dog again, Lucas was found alive—scrawny and shy, but very much alive.

His saga began in the fall of 1988 when he and his owner, Earl Cash, a self-employed contractor and Baptist minister in Pickens, South Carolina, were on a hunting trip in the wooded wilderness near Sudbury, Ontario. The hound spotted a black bear and chased him deep into the forest. Cash lost sight of the dog, but minutes later, he heard a painful yelp. "I heard him holler and I knew the bear had hit him or bit him," said Cash.

The owner spent the next five days scouring the woods in search of his prized dog. But he finally gave up and headed home without the pooch. The next year, Cash returned to the area and looked for his dog again. "I asked people if they had seen a black-and-tan hound," he recalled. "I got no results, so I just gave him up for dead."

Then, in February, 1992—three and a half years after he last saw Lucas—Cash received a phone call that left him thunderstruck. The call was from Jane Neve, an animal control officer from the town of Rayside-Balfour, Ontario. She told Cash she had a hound in her pound with a license tag that identified the canine as Lucas.

"I said, 'Say, what?'" recalled Cash. "And then she said he was a black-and-tan hound, and I knew she had my dog. I was very surprised, I guarantee you. I was speechless. I had given up all hope of ever seeing Lucas again. I just couldn't believe it."

For over a year before he was caught, Lucas would wander into the town, but never let people get too close to him. Lucas, whom residents nicknamed The Phantom, would forage through garbage cans for food and then scoot off into the woods only to return days or even weeks later. He was allowed to roam around town because he never bothered anyone.

But eventually, Neve felt it was best to catch him. She nabbed him when he fell asleep after eating canned cat food laced with a strong tranquilizer. Neve then brought Lucas to the animal shelter where she gave him a checkup. Other than being about ten pounds underweight, the dog was remarkably healthy.

With the information on the dog's tag, Neve contacted Cash with the stunning news.

"It's amazing that Lucas survived as he did because we often get temperatures as low as minus fifteen degrees up here," Neve told reporters. "In the summer, the mosquitoes are so bad even the moose come out of the bush to get into the wind."

A month after he was captured, Lucas, accompanied by Neve, flew back home to South Carolina on a trip paid for by the *Sudbury Star* newspaper. At the Greenville-Spartanburg Airport, Lucas arrived to a hero's welcome.

"You rascal, you," Cash said happily as he attached a yellow ribbon to the dog's collar and then gave him a big hug. Lucas remained quiet at first, somewhat stunned by all the attention. But within a matter of minutes, he perked up and nuzzled his owner.

"He recognized me," said Cash, beaming with joy. "I'm just so glad to have him back."

(Near) Death Trap

Sheba the Siberian husky was caught in a hunter's steel trap for thirteen excruciating days in bitter subzero cold, yet she still managed to survive.

Sheba lived with workers for a natural gas company in a remote camp 320 miles north of Edmonton, Alberta, Canada. One morning in 1991, she went out with one of the workers when she darted off into the woods, chasing a small animal. During her pursuit, she stepped into a trap and the steel jaws snapped shut on her right front paw. When Sheba didn't return, workers searched the woods for her, but to no avail.

"The crew thought she must have been killed by a bear," said Jerome Tangedal, a company supervisor.

But Sheba was alive, although she was fading fast. No matter how hard she struggled, she couldn't free herself from the trap's deadly jaws. Day after day, she grew weaker from hunger, pain, and the bone-numbing cold. But she didn't give up. She stayed alive by licking the snow and fending off wolves with her growls and barks.

Finally, thirteen long days after the trap had snared her, Sheba was found by gas worker Worley Rosson. He had gone out with another dog to check on a gas meter when his pooch began to bark. "Then I heard Sheba reply in a tiny, low whine," recalled Rosson. "I went rushing through the dense brush and there she was, about a quarter-mile away with her paw caught in a trap."

Rosson pried open the trap and brought Sheba back to the camp where he warmed her up and fed the famished dog all the food her stomach could hold. The dog had dropped in weight from 120 pounds down to ninety. Unfortunately, gangrene had set in her wounded leg and a few days later, her limb was amputated.

But a dog lover who learned about her brush with death carved a wooden peg and attached it to her stump with a bracket and two Velcro straps. Sheba adjusted to her artificial limb and was back trekking in the woods with her loving workers.

Said Tangedal, "Sheba has a heart as big as the great outdoors."

A Hole Lot of Trouble

Judy the Jack Russell terrier puppy disappeared down a rabbit hole and didn't come out until she was rescued—five weeks later!

In 1990, Evan Davies, eleven, of San Antonio, Texas, was walking Judy when she broke loose and chased a rabbit into its warren. Evan waited for his dog to return, but she didn't. The family assumed she somehow had died in the rabbit hole or had found another way out and was lost.

"Evan went out every day to the rabbit hole looking for Judy," his mother Jean told reporters. "Even though we'd all given up hope of ever seeing Judy again, Evan just wouldn't believe she was dead."

Finally, thirty-six days later, a neighbor walking by the rabbit hole heard a faint whimper coming from under the ground. So he got a shovel and began digging. Suddenly, out popped a dirty, skinny, brown-and-white puppy.

"It was Judy," recalled Evan. "I knew she was there somewhere, just waiting to be found. She was hungry and thirsty, but she was fine. She won't be going near any more holes."

Crime-Busting Dogs

...who took a bite out of lawbreakers

Nipping the 'Napper

An American spitz named Nori saved two little girls from the grasp of a kidnapper.

One day in 1991, Hannah Stubs and her friend Michel Felli, both two years old, were playing in the fenced backyard of Hannah's house in Colorado Springs, Colorado. Suddenly, a strange man approached the low fence and summoned the two toddlers. When they came over, he leaned over the fence, scooped up the girls, and took off running.

Hannah's mother Sharon had just stepped inside the house for a moment when the abduction occurred. She didn't see what had happened, but the family dog did.

"All of a sudden, Nori started growling and pawing at the door to get out," recalled Sharon. "When I went to pat her to tell her she couldn't go out, she turned and tried to bite me. That was very strange because Nori is normally very passive. So I said, 'Fine, go out.'

"I opened the door and Nori tore off down the porch and ran around the corner of the house, snarling the whole time. That's when I got a feeling something bad was happening. I ran after her and saw her jump the side fence."

Only then did Sharon realize a kidnapper had snatched Hannah and Michel and was running off with a helpless girl tucked under each arm.

Nori scampered several yards, then leaped and bit the abductor right in the seat of his pants. "He yelled in pain, shook off Nori, and dropped the girls in the next-door neighbor's yard," Sharon recalled. Fortunately, the frightened girls were safe and unharmed. But the suspect dashed off down the street and managed to elude the police.

"If it hadn't been for Nori, I shudder to think what might have happened," said Sharon. "She's amazing."

Mugging It Up

Sheena, a mixed-breed German shepherd, fought off a mugger after her handicapped owner was attacked.

One day in 1992, John Rayner, thirty-nine, of St. Petersburg, Florida, went grocery shopping and left his dog in the car. As he was returning to his auto, Rayner, who walks with a cane because of a back injury, was confronted by two thugs.

Sheena barked madly from inside the car as the punks took Rayner's wallet and demanded his watch. Rayner fought back, clubbing one of his attackers with his cane and knocking him out. But then the other mugger began beating up Rayner.

"I thought my life was over," the victim recalled. "He violently hit me in the chest and twisted me around so I was facing the car. I could hardly breathe. I knew right then he could stick a knife in me and kill me at any moment."

As he tried to protect himself, Rayner reached out with one hand and managed to open the car door. A split second later, Sheena leaped out of the auto.

"She hit the thug full in the chest and knocked him to the ground," Rayner recalled. "She was right in his face with her teeth. I could see he was terrified."

The robber fought Sheena and shoved her away before running off with the dog in hot pursuit. Rayner hobbled over to the store and called the police. By the time the cops arrived, Sheena had returned to the car, but both muggers had fled the scene.

Said Rayner, "I grabbed her beautiful big head and said, 'Thank you, Sheena. You saved my life.'"

For the canine hero, it was a payback. Four years earlier, the dog was a lonely stray that had been run over by a hit-and-run driver in front of Rayner's house. Rayner lovingly had nursed her back to health and given her a home.

Now it was Sheena's chance to return the favor.

A Gem of a Dog

Billon the German shepherd sniffed out and collared a gang of safecrackers who were trying to make off with $250,000 in gems in Manhattan in 1993.

Thanks to the efforts of the K-9 hero, police were able to solve a string of jewel heists involving millions of dollars worth of gems.

Billon put a bite on crime after three burglars broke into the eighth-floor offices of Citigold, Inc. Using a sophisticated electronic device, the intruders bypassed an alarm system. Then, wielding a blowtorch, they pierced through the five-inch-thick steel walls of the safe.

But then the thieves inadvertently triggered a second alarm—and minutes later, more than a dozen policemen surrounded the high-rise building. The burglars looked out the window, saw the cops below, and dropped a large black bag containing the quarter-million dollars in jewels. Then they fled out of the office and tried to hide inside the building.

Police launched a floor-by-floor search that they assumed would be long and painstaking. But then Billon was brought in to assist them. In minutes, the German shepherd sniffed out the suspects, even though they had thought they were safe from the cops by hiding behind ductwork inside a wall.

When Billon discovered them, one of the three suspects attempted to flee, but he didn't get very far. The growling dog dashed after the suspect, clamped his jaws around the man's leg, and held on until police handcuffed him. The other two burglars were so terrified of Billon that they surrendered immediately.

After the bust, his handler, Officer George O'Donnell, told reporters, "I'm calling Donald Trump's Edwardian Room restaurant for reservations and I'm buying Billon the biggest steak in the house."

Canine Collar

Barabus the police dog climbed up a ladder to a second-floor window and single-pawedly collared a burglary suspect.

The drama unfolded in 1991 after neighbors reported a break-in at an apartment in the Dorchester area of Boston. Arriving at the scene were Boston police K-9 Officer Raymond Armstead and his veteran canine companion, Barabus, an eight-year-old German shepherd.

Police quickly placed a ladder against an open second-floor window and sent Barabus to work. The dog, who had been trained to scale ladders and fire escapes, climbed up to the window and then crawled inside with Armstead right behind him.

Barabus then quickly searched the apartment, sniffing for signs of the suspect. Within a minute, he cornered the burglar hiding in the closet. When the suspect tried to bolt, the dog bit him on the leg and held him until police were able to arrest him.

"When we came out of the apartment building, we got a standing ovation from bystanders," Armstead recalled for reporters. "If we can put a stop to these burglaries, that's fantastic. That's what Barabus's job is all about."

The $3 Million Dog

No dog ever returned a bigger investment for the public than Prince.

The black German shepherd was purchased by the city of Lansing, Illinois, for $6,500 in April 1992. A year later, the dog discovered a treasure trove of drug money that poured more than $3 million into the city's coffers.

Prince and another drug-sniffing German shepherd had been bought by the town of thirty thousand people who were concerned about drug trafficking. "We're located just south of Chicago off Interstate 80," said Prince's handler Officer Dan Sylvester. "Couriers who carry drugs and drug money often spend the night in motels outside of Chicago, so the city thought it made sense to help fight the drug problem by getting the dogs.

"One day we got a call from a motel security guard that some people were acting nervous after they locked up their van in the parking lot. The van had no license plates. I took Prince to the van and he immediately alerted, which means he detected the scent of drugs." The sharp-nosed dog sat down and pointed his snout toward the back of the van. That was his signal that he smelled drugs.

"We quickly got a search warrant and when we looked inside, we found money everywhere—in shopping bags, garbage cans, and boxes," said Sylvester. "The money was wrapped in duct tape in $10,000 bundles. When we counted it all up, it totaled $5.2 million.

"We knew it had to be drug money because Prince is trained to smell drugs. The bills tested positive for traces of drugs. It's like a sweater left in a cedar chest. When you take it out, the sweater doesn't have any cedar chips on it, but it still has a slight smell of cedar."

If Prince hadn't alerted, the police wouldn't have had a reason to get a search warrant and examine the interior of the van. They never would have found the drug money.

Under state law, police confiscated the van and the cash, thanks to Prince's sensitive nose. "It was the largest seizure of drug money by a K-9 in Illinois history," said Sylvester. "In fact, it was the largest in about a ten-state area."

Following state law, Lansing got to keep 65 percent of the $5.2 million—about $3.38 million—which had to go for drug enforcement uses, while the rest of the money was shared by the county and state.

"We put the money in the bank and are using the interest to build a new police firing range and organize a drug-training program," said Sylvester.

"Prince turned out to be a heck of an investment. Dogs like him work cheap because he's happy just to get a treat or play with his tennis ball as a reward. He made a great pinch. He definitely earned his biscuits."

Dogging the Bad Guys

Ebony the black Labrador mix was an abandoned pup caged in an Illinois dog pound waiting to be put to sleep. But then U.S. Customs enlisted her in the war on drugs in 1988.

Ebony quickly began putting the collar on crooks and soon became the top dog in arrests and narcotic seizures in a special canine interdiction program at international airports and seaports across the country.

From 1988 to 1993, Ebony was responsible for over four hundred narcotic seizures worth over $100 million and three hundred arrests.

"She has always loved her work," said her handler, Ricky Grim, supervisory canine enforcement officer at Miami International Airport.

For years airports had been using German shepherds and Dobermans to sniff out concealed drugs in cargo, boxes, and suitcases. But then officials decided to use dogs to detect drugs smuggled in by arriving passengers. Realizing that big dogs would intimidate innocent passengers, officials began a program using smaller, friendlier dogs. Recruiting dogs from animal shelters, experts chose dogs with friendly temperaments and a willingness to learn. The dogs were sent to a facility in Front Royal, Virginia, for thirteen weeks of training. The passive dog detector program, as it's called, now has sixty-nine such canines on duty at various ports of entry.

These specially trained canines walk among arriving passengers who are clearing customs. If a dog detects drugs, he simply sits down at the smuggler's feet.

"A dog's nose is thousands of times more sensitive than a human's," said Grim. "For example, while we might smell beef stew as a single aroma, a dog will smell each individual ingredient—the beef, the carrots, the celery, the potatoes—and be trained to pick out only one of them."

After months of training, Ebony was one of the first dogs in the program to go on duty. Assigned to Miami, she quickly began making busts. "One time, a nicely dressed woman was standing in line at customs when Ebony walked by," recalled Grim. "The woman bent down and patted the dog and Ebony sat down—her signal to me that she had smelled a drug. We escorted the woman to a room where she was searched. A half-pound of cocaine was found hidden in her vagina.

"Another time a Haitian woman arrived at customs pushing a cart loaded with her luggage and a bucket full of cooked goat meat. Ebony sat down and at first we thought the dog was attracted to the goat meat. But Ebony seemed certain. So the woman was searched and a kilo of cocaine was found hidden in her bra."

Dogs such as Ebony often work about four hours a day and get a day off every seven to nine days. When they're not working, they live in kennels at the airport. Their reward for making a bust is a chance to play with a rolled-up terry cloth towel.

"When Ebony goes to work, she roars out of the kennel," said Grim. "She's proud and very energetic. She and the other dogs in the program compete with each other. To them, finding drugs on people is just a big game and they enjoy it. We have a nickname for Ebony. We call her 'No. 1.' That's because she's the top dog in the country."

* * *

For five years, Corky the beagle was a flop as a drug-sniffing pooch. He didn't find any dope at all and was nearly discharged from the U.S. Navy.

But then, after he was turned over to a new trainer and handler, Corky became the Navy's top dog, helping nab nearly five hundred drug users in two years. He was so good that in 1990 he received a commendation from First Lady Barbara Bush.

From 1983 to 1988, Corky went around military bases, trying to sniff out drugs and help make busts. But the only bust was Corky. Frustrated officials turned the dud of a doggy detective over to veteran trainer Joe Pastella and handler Burton Hunt. They sharpened Corky's skills by hiding drugs and then rewarding him with treats, hugs, and lots of love whenever he found the drugs. The results were amazing.

"Soon he was nosing out dope in roofs, people's pockets, cars, buildings, anywhere," Hunt told reporters. "He even jumped on a guy's desk and found a tiny amount of cocaine hidden under a book."

In one of his best busts of all, Corky signaled that he had sniffed drugs that were still inside a locked car. Military police examined the car's interior but found nothing. "Finally, they said, 'Your dog must be wrong,'" recalled Hunt. "But I said, 'Corky's never wrong.'"

Corky went inside the car and immediately headed for the backseat and began pawing behind it. When the MPs removed the seat, they found a small bag of cocaine hidden underneath.

Said Hunt, "Corky makes a believer out of everyone."

Beagle Scouts

Government dogs sniff out more than just drugs.

The United States Department of Agriculture runs the Beagle Brigade, a canine unit that detects forbidden fresh fruits, vegetables, and meat products carried by travelers who knowingly or unknowingly violate customs regulations.

Formed in 1986, the Beagle Brigade monitors international flights entering the country. Beagles were chosen for the job because of their docile nature, keen sense of smell, and nonthreatening presence. Each dog strolls through the baggage claim area with a handler. If the beagle detects any agricultural contraband, he signals by sitting with his head erect. The baggage and the person who owns it are then brought to a customs office for inspection and questioning.

"The beagles are truly incredible," said Hal Fingerman, regional program coordinator. "One of our dogs signaled a single clove of garlic, wrapped in a sealed plastic bag, located in the center of a large trunk. Another dog keyed on lemons carried in a bottle of water inside a large, hard suitcase."

Dogs also have been trained to smell out deer, elk, moose, and even salmon. But these canines are not friends of hunters and fishermen. Quite the contrary.

Various state conservation officers use the dogs to detect the spoils of poachers and illegal anglers. The dogs will walk around vehicles at various checkpoints and sniff for illegal meat and catches.

Hunter of Lost Dogs

Sadie Sue is a working bloodhound. But she doesn't track down criminals or missing children. Instead, she's trained to hunt for one thing—lost dogs.

"She's the only one of her kind now working," said her owner, W.R. "Bill" Bailey, of Albuquerque, New Mexico. Sadie Sue is following in the footsteps of Bailey's first dog-tracking bloodhound, also named Sadie Sue, who worked on dozens of cases before succumbing to cancer in 1991.

"I just thought there was a need for a dog to track missing dogs," explained Bailey who trained both Sadie Sues to track only other canines. A bloodhound can pick up a scent from a mile away as well as one that's several days old. To track a dog, the blood-hound first needs to sniff something that carries the canine's scent, such as a piece of cloth from his bed, a toy, or a collar.

"We had one case—a farmer's missing black dog—where Sadie Sue Number One didn't have anything to work with," recalled Bailey. "So we had the owner use tweezers and collect dog hair from the sofa. Once we had enough, I put them in a plastic bag and let Sadie Sue get a good sniff. Then she went running off down into a ditch, past a cow pen and a hog pen on another farm. When she reached some bushes, she stopped and pointed. We found the dog. Unfortunately, he had been shot to death.

"One of the funniest cases we had came after I got a frantic call from a couple who said their dog was missing. They had looked everywhere for over a day. Well, Sadie Sue Number One quickly picked up a scent and kept circling the house. Then she scratched at the front door. We opened the door and she went into the house and found the dog right away. It had been inside the whole time!

"When the first Sadie Sue died, I knew I wanted to carry on the tradition," said Bailey. "I believe there is a need for this."

Sadie Sue Number Two has helped owners recover dogs that had been stolen.

"One time, she tracked a scent to a construction site and zeroed in on a certain worker who denied any knowledge about the missing dog," said Bailey. "We questioned him a lot and we were convinced he had the dog. He panicked. The next day, someone just happened to drop the dog off at the local animal shelter. We knew it was the guy but we couldn't prove it. But at least the owners got their dog back."

In another case, a distraught couple flew Bailey and Sadie Sue to San Jose, California, to find their missing Yorkshire terrier who had wandered away after squirming through a broken backyard fence. "Sadie Sue tracked the dog to a park about three-quarters of a mile away," recalled Bailey. "But then the scent just stopped. I knew then that the dog had been picked up by someone. So we spread the word with the media and she was eventually returned."

Not all cases end successfully. "Many times, it's obvious that the dog had been stolen and there's no way to track the animal down," said Bailey. "Usually, it's a show dog. Sometimes people will see a friendly dog in a nice area and steal it and then wait to see if the owner offers a reward for the dog's return."

Bailey and Sadie Sue track only for expense money. When they're not working together, Bailey teams up with his other bloodhound, Mortimer, who is trained for the search and rescue of people. They are members of a volunteer group that works with the New Mexico State Department of Public Safety.

"Sadie Sue and I really enjoy trying to find lost dogs," said Bailey. "When we do find a dog, the owners are elated. They can't do enough for me. Their excitement makes it all worthwhile."

Astounding Dogs

...who performed amazing feats

Duke's Ups and Downs

Life was a roller coaster for Duke the standard poodle.

Every day for nearly six years, he rode a wild amusement park roller coaster called the Skyliner. With his ears flapping and fur flying, he hurtled up and down the slopes and screeched around hairpin turns at a blood-rushing sixty-five miles an hour.

The champagne-colored dog also enjoyed the Ferris wheel, the Octopus, and the fast-spinning Tilt-A-Whirl, all at Lakemont Park in Altoona, Pennsylvania.

"He was a canine thrill-seeker," said his owner John Eichelberger, director of maintenance for the park. "He just loved amusement rides. He couldn't get enough of them."

Eichelberger, who grew up working in carnivals, said that Duke was addicted to the excitement of the rides ever since he was a puppy. "He used to bark at the Ferris wheel, so I finally took him up and he loved it," said his owner. "I'd see him go off on his own and hop on a spinning merry-go-round. He'd even stand in line, hoping someone would take him back up on the Ferris wheel."

In 1988, Eichelberger quit the nomadic carnival life for a permanent job at Lakemont Park, where Duke became famous as the daredevil dog who made a daily routine of hopping aboard amusement rides. "Duke usually began his day by taking a swim in the park's lake," said Eichelberger. "Then he would jump out of the water and run over to the Skyliner, which we tested every morning before the park opened.

"I didn't strap him in. He would put his front paws over the bar and then brace his feet in the corner. I would sit next to him, ready to grab him if we came to a sudden stop or if he lost his footing. He loved every second of it.

"Then he would follow me to the next ride to be tested that morning. He'd jump onto a seat in the Ferris wheel and bark until I turned it on and got it going.

"The dog simply loved thrills and motion. He would go down the park's water slide on his belly and sometimes he'd go on fast, spinning rides. When he got off them, he'd stagger for a bit and have to sit until he got his balance—much like humans do after one of those rides."

Duke managed to coax extra rides on the roller coaster by hanging around the loading area. "Everyone wanted to take him up with them. We let him ride with kids only on special occasions, such as a terminally ill child on an outing or a church group," said his owner. "Duke made all kids—and adults—happy. He had a great personality."

Duke died at the age of twelve in 1993. "It's been over a year and I still haven't gotten used to his death," admitted Eichelberger. "Duke was one in a million."

The Long Walk Home

An old, nearly deaf dog who was lost trekked twenty-two miles in twenty-four days through bitter cold without food or shelter—but finally made it back to her loving home.

The incredible journey of thirteen-year-old Kokomo began the day after Christmas in 1993 when owner Terry Powers, of West Islip, Long Island, New York, dropped the dog off at his parents' house in East Meadow for what was supposed to be a one-night visit.

"They let her out near midnight and she jumped the fence and disappeared," recalled Powers. "She used to live there years ago when she was a puppy so she probably wanted to visit some old friends. Unfortunately, she got lost."

Days passed. Then weeks. Temperatures had dropped into the single digits at night with wind chill factors of twenty below. Days were windy, bleak, and snowy.

"I kept looking out my window and saying, 'Please come home, Kokomo,' but you really don't expect it to happen," said Powers's wife Carolyn.

99

The Powerses drove along the shoreline, asking people if they had seen an old brown mixed-breed dog that looked lost. The answer was always no until the third week when someone spotted Kokomo two towns away. Acting on a suggestion from an animal expert, the Powerses slept with scarves and then left them along a route from their house to the spot where the dog had been sighted. The couple hoped that Kokomo would pick up the scent of one of the scarves.

Whether it was the scarves or the dog's remarkable determination, the moment the Powerses had been so desperately waiting for arrived on the twenty-fourth day of Kokomo's disappearance. "It was at 3:30 in the morning," recalled Powers. "We heard a bark outside. Carolyn ran to the front door and she screamed. I grabbed a baseball bat and ran over to her, not knowing what was happening. And there was Kokomo."

The dog limped into the house and was weak and tired. The Powerses took her to the vet who discovered that Kokomo suffered a major hip dislocation from a possible accident and had lost a third of her body weight. Despite her age—the equivalent of ninety-one in humans—Kokomo was otherwise in fairly good shape.

"It's amazing," said Carolyn. "You hear stories like this, and you want to believe them. Now I can."

Top Dogs

The town of Guffey, Colorado, has a bitch of a mayor—a friendly golden retriever named Shanda.

She was elected on a voice vote in 1993 and is the latest four-legged mayor to hold the top post in the tiny unincorporated town forty-five miles west of Colorado Springs. Since 1987, Guffey, population thirty-five, had elected cats for its last three mayors. But then along came Shanda.

"The town needed a change," said Shanda's owner, Dawn Buffington, who along with her husband Bruce runs the Guffey General Store and Bootlegger Spirits. "When we bought the store in 1993, the cat who used to be mayor retired. So we thought Shanda deserved a chance and the people around here agreed. Besides, the cat was a Democrat and Shanda is a Republican."

The mayor, who uses the store as her office, has her own bodyguard—an Akita named Tojo. "But Shanda is pretty popular, so Tojo has an easy job," said Dawn.

Shanda, who always sports either a red or black bandana around her neck, is willing to wag her tail and lick the feet of her constituents when they come calling. And she's more than willing to act as the town's ambassador. "People come from all over the country to see our mayor," said Dawn. "They want to have their picture taken with her and she loves it. She's so easy-going. I think she'll be a mayor for a long, long time."

★ ★ ★

The dog who held the office of mayor the longest was a part–black Labrador, part–Rottweiler named Bosco. He was top dog in the small town of Sunol, California, for ten years.

Bosco became the mayor of the unincorporated town of 1,500 residents in 1981 when a dozen people were sitting at a local bar, complaining about the lack of elected officials in Sunol. Two men said they wouldn't mind being mayor, so the bar patrons decided to vote by a show of hands.

"Just before we were about to vote, somebody laughingly nominated Bosco," recalled the dog's owner Tom Stillman. "His self-appointed campaign manager came up with a three-point campaign: a cat in every tree, a bone in every dish, and a fire hydrant on every street corner."

Finding those promises appealing, the patrons voted overwhelmingly for Bosco as their first mayor. For the next ten years, he spent his days walking around town like a true politician, visiting the local café, grocery store, and post office. Occasionally, he accepted handouts, but his constituents didn't mind. He performed his biggest duty every Halloween.

That's when Bosco would wear a red satin bow around his neck and lead the town's annual parade.

In 1987, the responsibility of his office apparently became too much for Bosco to bear and he disappeared. Concerned townspeople put out fliers, called local media, and searched the nearby woods without success. But six days later, Bosco strolled back into town and resumed his mayoral duties until age finally caught up with him.

Bark if You Want to be President

In the 1980s, there were presidential candidates who weren't afraid to admit they were dogs.

That's because they *were* dogs.

A black Labrador named Windi April Reedy actually registered with the Federal Election Commission for a run at the White House in 1984. "She filed for president and she sent in the correct forms," said her campaign manager, Gil Campbell. "She even put her paw print where the signature should go, and the forms were accepted."

Windi's biggest problem, aside from being a dog, was her age. She was only nine and the law says candidates for president must be at least thirty-five years old.

Although she truly had a leg up on the competition, Windi didn't capture many votes.

Four years later, another candidate bristling with animal magnetism was duly registered with the Federal Election Commission as a candidate for the White House. He was Punch Burger, an eight-year-old half–German shepherd, half–keeshond.

Punch tossed his leash into the political arena as a protest against the usual poor quality of officeseekers, according to his owner, Laura Van Sant, of Chapel Hill, North Carolina. Punch made appearances around town and on television and national magazines. He ran on a platform of fewer import restrictions on beef.

Alluding to the scandal surrounding one of the two-legged candidates, Laura told reporters, "Punch is no Gary Hart. He was neutered at six months."

Tiny Dog Makes Big News

There's a reason why Thumbelina was named after the teeny-weeny girl in the Hans Christian Andersen fairy tale.

The Yorkshire terrier is considered the smallest adult dog in the world. She stretches just eight inches long from nose to tail and stands five and a half inches high—small enough to fit into a coffee mug. At sixteen ounces before meals, Thumbelina weighs two ounces less than the previous recordholder, a tiny Chihuahua.

Owned by Maureen Howes, a breeder of Yorkshire terriers in Worcestershire, England, the tiny pooch simply stopped growing a month after she was born in 1992. A veterinarian who examined Thumbelina said she is perfectly healthy and has stunted growth because of a genetic problem.

Marathon Mutt

Velia, a German shorthaired pointer, became the first dog to finish a world-class 3,000-mile endurance run.

She wound up in the strenuous international event after acting as coach for her mistress, Mary Margaret Goodwin.

The fifty-one-year-old runner said that without her canine coach, she wouldn't have been able to complete the grueling Trans-Himalayan Ultra Run from Nepal to India in 1988. During the five months she spent training for the event, Goodwin relied on Velia to be her pacer.

Goodwin was given Velia because the pointer's original owners couldn't control Velia's constant running.

"Velia was a terrific coach," she said. "In the mornings, she would nag me to get up and get going. On the trail, she'd bark and stomp her feet if she got ahead and wanted me to pick up the pace."

Because Velia loved to run, she joined Goodwin in the endurance race. During the torturous Ultra Run, Goodwin carried daily food and other on-trail supplies while porters traveling by jeep brought the rest of the gear. Often, the porters located Goodwin and Velia by asking villagers, "Where's the American lady with a dog?"

Goodwin recalled that as many as two hundred people would watch her set up camp at the end of each day. "Nobody there had ever seen a shorthaired dog," she said, "so many of them asked what it was. Some even asked if Velia was a tiger."

Climbing up and over mountain peaks, splashing through monsoons, and running in stifling heat, Goodwin and her pooch averaged thirty-five miles a day on roads and about twenty miles on trails. The determined runner finished in 170 days and became the first woman ever to complete the arduous course—and Velia became the world's first dog to accomplish the same feat.

The Nose Knows

Dogs have been sticking their noses in Canada's largest oil company—and saving it millions of dollars.

A division of Imperial Oil Limited is tracing pipeline leaks with trained Labrador retrievers who have proven to be far more accurate than sophisticated equipment.

The dogs sniff for a miniscule amount of an odorous chemical added to oil and natural gas in pipelines, locating pinhead-sized leaks up to eighteen feet below ground.

"When all of the usual technology failed us, we had to come up with something new," said Ron Quaife, manager of international technology marketing for Canada's largest oil and natural gas company.

Quaife's team developed a chemical that rises from a leak straight through the ground. But finding a way to detect small amounts of the chemical proved difficult. The most sensitive laboratory equipment was not sensitive enough and proved too fragile and expensive. Some of the devices cost up to $800 million to develop—and as much as $30,000 per mile of pipe to operate.

Imperial was searching for a cost-effective detector when Quaife became intrigued with Canada Customs' use of dogs that sniff out illegal drugs and goods at airports. He conducted several tests on Labradors to see if they could detect pipeline leaks and they passed with flying colors.

By the end of 1993, a team of seventeen Labs had found 134 out of 136 gas leaks—and at only a quarter of the cost of mechanical systems.

The Dogs of War

During the Gulf War in 1991, French forces used dogs as "mobile radars."

A French Air Force division of nearly 1,200 highly trained German shepherds flawlessly carried out its mission to patrol the grounds near French Jaguar fighter planes. "The dogs served their country well," declared Alain Colorado, commander of the canine division.

The dogs, who learned the scent of their human comrades-in-arms, could sniff out an impostor in the ranks up to thirty-six hours after an intrusion. The dogs also were trained to have a nose for explosives.

Throughout the Gulf War, no one from the enemy ever penetrated the French air base.

Mail Pooch

A letter carrier in the French town of Berne doesn't need a mail pouch. That's because he uses a mail pooch.

In 1989, Cosak the German shepherd began making the rounds with his master, mailman Jean François Pichon. The dog would run alongside Pichon's bicycle. But the dog soon wanted to become more involved.

"He was begging for me to give him parcels and letters to carry in his mouth," Pichon said in a magazine interview. But the mailman found that method was too sloppy, so he had a backpack with large pockets made for Cosak to carry.

Loaded up with as much as thirty pounds of mail, Cosak goes from house to house in the village of 1,500 people. When houses have a gate, Cosak jumps up on it and pushes the bell with his paw. He walks to the front door and barks to let residents know the mail pooch has arrived.

The occupants take only the mail addressed to them out of his backpack. Sometimes they give him a treat in return.

"He loves his job," said Pichon. "If for any reason I couldn't go on my rounds, Cosak would be capable to continue by himself."

* * *

A dog in the small town of Dyer, Tennessee, knows the mail route so well that he has helped train new letter carriers.

Since 1987, a white mutt named Squirt has shown a passion for the U.S. Postal Service. Most every day, he waits at the post office for one of the carriers to begin the route. When the carrier heads out in the truck, the dog walks ahead and escorts the carrier. Then, when the carrier gets out to walk part of the route, Squirt proudly leads the way with his bushy tail wagging in the breeze.

No one knows why the dog has such a fondness for postal workers. "The mailman petted him one day and it all started," said Jesse Fletcher, who along with his parents, Terry and Debbie, own Squirt.

For Dyer's mail carriers, Squirt is a mascot and a daily companion. The dog knows all the routes in this small town of 2,500 people. Because of his familiarity with the routes, the dog has helped new carriers find their way around the area.

When mail carrier Jane Allen first began walking the route in Dyer, she just strapped on her bag and let Squirt lead the way. He even showed her a few shortcuts.

"He's our mascot and a daily companion," said postmaster Charles Tyner. "He's also the biggest celebrity in town."

The Termite Terminator

For years, Danny the beagle has been the terror of termites.

The dog sniffs out the wood-chomping bugs for a pest control company—with incredible results.

"Danny hasn't been wrong yet," declared Jeffrey Smith, sales and marketing manager for Dallas Pest & Termite Co., in Dallas, Texas. "He eliminates all the guesswork. Humans need to see evidence of termites. But Danny can hear and smell them."

To find termites, exterminators use a flashlight and a screwdriver to probe the wood. But the painstaking task is not always accurate. However, Danny's supersensitive nose and ears have helped him discover where termites are hiding. The bug-busting dog can detect the scent given off by termites. He also can hear them when their jaws vibrate.

Danny, who was trained to sniff out termites, began working in 1986 at the age of two for the exterminating firm which paid a whopping $20,000 for him.

"He's worth every cent," said Smith, whose company charges customers $250 for Danny to poke his nose around their house. "Danny inspects fifteen to twenty houses a week and he's remarkably accurate. Our customers love him."

When he's not working, Danny takes on the role of the family beagle for company employee Brad Pitts, his wife, and their three children. Pitts is Danny's handler whenever they go on a job together.

"When Danny hears termites, he'll suddenly stop, cock his head, and perk his ears," said Pitts. "He'll go over, smell the area, and alert me that the termites are there by pawing the ground. He gets so excited. He looks back at me and his little tail goes back and forth like a windshield wiper.

"We once hid dishes of termites in a house under construction in all sorts of hard-to-find places—and Danny found every single one. He just loves to find termites."

Dog Lovers

...who truly were a dog's best friend

Bad Pipe Dreams

When Aaron Gonzalez's seven puppies had fallen down a sewer pipe in his backyard, he was determined to do whatever it took to save them. It meant digging up his yard, ruining his plumbing system, and flooding his home.

But, he said, it was worth it.

The ordeal unfolded on a Sunday morning in 1992 when the puppies' frantic mother, Girl, began barking and whining in the yard. "She was crying," Aaron recalled. "She was telling us something was wrong."

When Aaron and his wife Sharon went to investigate, they discovered that their half-chow, half-huskie mother dog had knocked off the cover to a four-inch trap line leading to the family's sewer pipe. Her seven two-week-old pups had fallen in. With her slender arm, Sharon managed to pull out only two of them.

Aaron then dug several feet to where the pipe ran horizontally toward the house and cracked open the line. As a result, he lost his sewer and water service and flooded his bathroom. To make matters worse, he still couldn't reach the other dogs. And they were so frightened they wouldn't come when the frantic couple kept calling to them.

In desperation, Aaron turned to the city for help, but none of the agencies he called would come out. So he came up with a new idea. He borrowed his neighbor's shop vacuum and managed to suck three more pups safely from the pipe.

By now it was 2 A.M. and the couple had rescued five of the seven puppies. Exhausted, the Gonzalezes called it quits for the night. "But we couldn't sleep because the trapped puppies cried and cried and their whimpering mother refused to leave the hole," Aaron recalled. "It was ugly."

The couple's heart broke to see Girl camped by the hole all night long, whimpering for her remaining lost puppies.

The next morning, Aaron tried the city again. He got only this cold-hearted advice: Chop up the pups with a plumber's snake and flush them away. "They wanted me to take the easy way out, but I couldn't do that," he said.

His neighbor, Jose Perez, then persuaded their city councilman to use some clout. A few hours later, fifteen city workers showed up with a backhoe and dug a trench to the pipe below.

The workers reached one of the puppies but it had died. However, after another couple of hours, a worker snagged the other mud-covered puppy with a length of stiff clothesline. When the filthy dog was freed, an elated Aaron give him to Perez who declared, "I'm going to call him Stinky."

Meanwhile, the Gonzalezes were left with a flooded house, no water or sewer service, and ruined tile and carpeting—over $1,000 in damage. They didn't have the money to cover it. "We didn't think about how to pay for the repairs until the puppies were safe," said Sharon. "Then we looked at each other and said, 'What do we do now?'"

Their worries were short-lived. When their heartwarming story was reported on local television and in the newspaper, retailers and fellow animal lovers donated money, time, and supplies to the Gonzalezes. One person dropped by with a playpen for the puppies while another brought dog food. Kirstie Alley, who starred in the hit TV sitcom "Cheers," called the couple to offer her admiration and a check to cover the cost of the remaining repairs.

"We are so very grateful to everyone," said Sharon, who helped find good homes for all the puppies. Added Aaron, "It was worth it to see those dogs come out alive."

Signs of Love

Juliette, a deaf Dalmatian, had been given up as a lost cause because she was uncontrollable. But then she was adopted by a loving family who finally trained her—by teaching her American Sign Language.

Now she's a sweet, lovable family pet who's considered the first deaf canine to learn ASL.

About 30 percent of all Dalmatians are born deaf in one or both ears because of a hereditary defect. Juliette was one of those dogs and her deafness caused her to misbehave as a puppy.

On two occasions, the dog had been adopted out of an animal shelter in Spokane, Washington. But both times, she was returned because her new families couldn't handle her bad behavior. So the year-old dog remained in a kennel cage with a sign that read: "Deaf—Cannot be controlled."

But then Michael and Jody Eisenman and their two children, Aaron and J.J., decided to take a chance with her. "Knowing she was deaf and had some behavior problems only served as a challenge," said Jody.

And what a challenge Juliette was. The dog would jump over furniture and onto the dinner table to help herself to a meal. She dug in the trash and chewed up toys and library books. "She was really difficult the first couple of weeks," said Jody. "We had trouble getting her attention."

As luck would have it, the family had taken classes in ASL, even though none are hearing impaired. So they began teaching Juliette sign language. The first signs she learned were "no" and "sit." The family would sign "no" if she had misbehaved and then "sit" to help focus her attention on them. Juliette slowly began to respond.

Over the next three years, she learned more than thirty signs, including "I love you," "home," "food," "out," "hungry," "play ball," "good girl," "lie down," and "go for a walk."

Terry Ryan, an internationally known dog obedience instructor, told the *Seattle Times* that he had never heard of a deaf dog learning ASL. "It doesn't surprise me," he said. "Humans routinely underestimate what dogs can do."

Kiss of Life

A K-9 officer saved the life of his police dog when she stopped breathing—by giving the pooch mouth-to-nose resuscitation.

Officer John Bassler, a trainer at the Pittsburgh Police K-9 School, was at home with his Belgian Malinois named Heidi one day in 1991 when she came bounding down the stairs with two rubber balls in her mouth. Suddenly, she stopped and appeared to be in distress.

"I could tell she was choking, so I opened her mouth and got one of the balls out," recalled Bassler. "But the other one was lodged deep in her throat. It was too slippery to grab.

"I turned to my brother Jim and said, 'She's going down!' Then she lost consciousness. While Jim kept her mouth open, I reached in with one hand. With the other hand, I massaged the outside of her throat, trying to push the ball up. I finally got it out. But by now she wasn't breathing and I couldn't detect a heartbeat.

"I closed her mouth, put my mouth over her nose and gave her three good breaths. Meanwhile, Jim was doing some chest compressions. Suddenly, I saw her eyes blink and within a couple of minutes, she had regained consciousness and was breathing fine. She was dazed for quite a while though, but otherwise okay.

"I just did what I had to do. I didn't want to lose her."

* * *

A thirteen-year-old boy used the Heimlich maneuver to save the life of his cocker spaniel when she choked on a piece of a rawhide bone.

Justin Weigel, of Lawrence, Kansas, had learned the Heimlich maneuver in an American Red Cross course. "They didn't say anything about using it on dogs," he said. On New Year's Day, 1991, he put his life-saving knowledge to work.

His two-year-old dog Muffie was choking to death. "I opened her mouth," he told reporters. "I couldn't see anything, but her gums and tongue were blue. I knew I had to do something fast or she would die."

So he wrapped his arms around Muffie's stomach and sat down on the porch steps. Making a ball with his hands, he put them below her ribs and squeezed about a half-dozen times. "Suddenly Muffie coughed and out came this piece of rawhide," he said.

The dog had been chewing on a two-inch-thick knob off the end of a rawhide bone when she tried to swallow it. The piece became stuck in her throat until Justin dislodged it. Once she was able to breathe again, she recovered quickly.

For his efforts, Justin received an award from the local American Red Cross chapter. He was given a certificate of recognition for "extraordinary action" in using his skills to save a life.

Legal Beagle

Linda Cawley is one rrrruff attorney—she specializes in dog law.

"I'm pretty sure I'm the first, if not the only, attorney who specializes in canine litigation," the Denver lawyer said proudly. Her clients are often dog owners who want to defend their pets in a criminal matter or be compensated when they believe their pets have died through the fault of others.

"People get emotionally attached to dogs because of their pets' unwavering loyalty and undivided love," said Cawley. "One man told me, 'Women come and go, but my dog remains the same.' People fight for their dogs because their pets can't speak up for themselves."

At any given time, Cawley has 150 cases in progress throughout the country. Among the cases: dogs caught in custody battles, overdue dog-support payments, trust funds for canines, dogs who made unwanted sexual advances on other dogs, canines lost by airlines, dogs accused of attacking someone, and wrongful death. Legal costs range from $1,500 to $5,000 and can double if the case goes to trial.

"With wrongful deaths, I often deal with insurance companies that take the position a dog is property and its owner isn't entitled to compensation for emotional distress. They know better than to go to trial with me."

In one California case, Cawley won $22,000 from a veterinarian's insurance company to compensate for the emotional suffering of the owner of an ailing dog that had died at the animal clinic. The vet failed to take X-rays that would have revealed the cause of the dog's troubles—it had swallowed a tennis ball.

Cawley represented the accused in a dog rape case in South Carolina. A golden retriever was ready to mate with a male of the same breed when a black Labrador got there first. When the retriever gave birth to mixed-breed puppies, her owner sued the Lab's master. "I was called in and managed to get a reduced settlement," Cawley recalled.

She's often retained when a dog gets caught in the middle of a nasty divorce. "One time a California couple battled over custody of their Airedale. The husband dog-napped their pet to Nevada and then hired me. I worked out an arrangement where the ex-wife got the dog back but the former husband was allowed visitation rights."

In one of her strangest cases, Cawley represented a Chicago woman who was so nuts about poodles she lived with an astounding 140 of them. The woman was charged with a city zoning violation for having too many dogs. "I helped arrange for her to move to a ranch in Colorado where she could keep all her precious poodles," said Cawley.

Then there was the time Cawley defended a nuisance barker—not a dog, but a man. In Lakewood, Colorado, a man was in his backyard when the neighbor's dog barked at him. So the man barked back and the two engaged in a little barking war. "Incredibly, he was charged with animal cruelty for harassing the dog," said Cawley. "The case actually went to court. I fought the charge as a freedom of speech issue. The judge ruled not guilty."

Cawley, a dog lover who owns a German shepherd named Dar and a Shiloh shepherd named Tucker, began practicing dog law in 1988 after she helped breeders rework their contracts. "I always wanted to be a lawyer and I always loved dogs," she said. "But I never thought I'd put the two together."

No More Dog Days for this Canine

A German shepherd named Gunther III became the richest pooch in the world when he inherited a whopping $65 million in 1992.

But before the dog can get his paws on the fortune, he will have to wait out the results of a bitter legal battle.

In the late 1980s, wealthy German countess Carlotta Liebenstein, an eccentric dog lover, was mesmerized by a novelty record called "Wild Dog" that featured the howls of a German shepherd named Gunther. Although the song was not a big hit in Europe, the countess loved it. In fact, she was so enamored by the dog that she traveled to Gunther's home in Fauglia, Italy, a small village near Pisa, just to meet him in person.

While she was there, Carlotta met Gunther's son, a frisky purebred named Gunther III, who instantly captured the elderly woman's heart. "She fell in love with Gunther III," his owner, Maurizio Mian, told reporters. "She bought a house near here and would always be with Gunther III, taking him for walks."

She spent her final days with Gunther III before she died of breast cancer. Carlotta had no immediate family. Her only son—who, ironically, was named Gunther—was killed in an auto accident in 1989. So she bequeathed her entire fortune to Gunther III under the legal banner of the Gunther Foundation Trust headed by his master.

"She was so disappointed that no one else liked the song 'Wild Dog' that she decided to leave her money to help others understand animals," said Mian.

But the countess's relatives howled in protest and have challenged the dog and his owner in court over Carlotta's will.

Unfazed, Mian told reporters Gunther III's inheritance "was a wonderful and extravagant gesture by the old lady. She loved Gunther III and he made her last years happy."

★ ★ ★

Since 1987, two dogs have lived alone in a furnished three-bedroom, $100,000 house—following the wishes of their late owner.

In the mid-1980s, Helen Walsh of Memphis, Tennessee, took in two stray puppies, Nickie and Carla, and gave them a loving home—literally. The elderly woman lived alone and enjoyed the canine company. They would watch television together and sleep together. But in 1987, Helen died.

"The dogs gave her so much happiness that she couldn't bear to think of them alone and miserable after she passed away," Helen's niece, Sister Mary Michael Greaber, told reporters. "To ease her mind, she left enough money to provide them with food and veterinary care as long as they live." After the dogs die, the house will be sold with the money going to charity.

Meanwhile, Sister Mary stops by the lovely brick house twice a day to feed and walk the dogs and make sure they are okay. "To be perfectly honest, a lot of humans don't live as well as Nickie and Carla," said the nun. "But anybody who knows these two dogs can't begrudge them a thing. They're two of the most lovable pets in the world."